"Tails" of the Afterlife
True Stories of Ghost Pets

Peggy Schmidt

Schiffer Publishing Ltd

4880 Lower Valley Road, Atglen, Pa 19310

Schiffer Books are available at special discounts for bulk purchases for sales promotions or premiums. Special editions, including personalized covers, corporate imprints, and excerpts can be created in large quantities for special needs. For more information contact the publisher:

Published by Schiffer Publishing Ltd.
4880 Lower Valley Road
Atglen, PA 19310
Phone: (610) 593-1777; Fax: (610) 593-2002
E-mail: Info@schifferbooks.com

For the largest selection of fine reference books on this and related subjects, please visit our web site at **www.schifferbooks.com**
We are always looking for people to write books on new and related subjects. If you have an idea for a book please contact us at the above address.

This book may be purchased from the publisher.
Include $5.00 for shipping.
Please try your bookstore first.
You may write for a free catalog.

In Europe, Schiffer books are distributed by
Bushwood Books
6 Marksbury Ave.
Kew Gardens
Surrey TW9 4JF England
Phone: 44 (0) 20 8392-8585; Fax: 44 (0) 20 8392-9876
E-mail: info@bushwoodbooks.co.uk
Website: www.bushwoodbooks.co.uk
Free postage in the U.K., Europe; air mail at cost.

Designed by RoS
Type set in Bickley Script LET/Schneidler BT
ISBN: 978-0-7643-3253-1

Printed in China

Acknowledgments

Special thanks to:
My family, friends, and office staff who shared
their stories and their constant love and support
with me.
Peggy, Terry, and Spectres Belgian Sheepdogs,
who shared so much time and so many stories.
Oakes K9 Dog Training for their help in securing
the wonderful dog pictures that appear in this
book.
Delaware Valley Golden Retriever Rescue for
the Golden Pictures.
Francine and her Rhodesian Ridgebacks, Reno,
Soxie, and Sage.
All Creatures Great and Small Pet Sitting for
their advice and stories.
My business partner, Andrea, for working with
me in this paranormal world.
The Blumenstock family, the most dedicated
animal lovers that I know.
D. P. Roseberry, my editor, who always had
great ideas.

♥ Contents

Introduction

Tough Beginnings

As one of the owners of Ghost Tours of America, I am always on the lookout for a good ghost story. It seemed logical to me, since there is an animal story in every one of our tours, that there had to be many out there. However, as I began writing this book, I found it extremely difficult for even the most devoted pet owner to share a story.

People were embarrassed to admit that they experienced a fleeting glance of their deceased pet at the door or the feeling of that little bundle of fur on their bed. They would deny they heard the jingle of their pet's collar or their footsteps on the stairs. They even tried to explain away the warning *woof* when they were in trouble. Since pet owners are often ridiculed when they grieve for a pet, what would people think of them if they believed they saw and possibly communicated with their deceased pet's spirit?

But I knew that there had to be owners out there who would be willing to talk. So I decided to visit some local dog shows. After limited success, I finally attended a large national dog show in order to interview a large cross section of dog owners. My technique of beginning the conversation with "Can I ask you a strange question?" eliminated the fear that they would appear foolish.

Some of the stories told to me were so heartwarming; they made me cry along with the owner who was telling it. Many times, the pet had been gone for years, but stories of their ghost returning made their owners smile and sometimes cry.

As I wrote this book, I read and reread the stories many

times, and to this day, some of the stories still bring tears to my eyes. You will notice that there are numerous similarities in the stories even if the dog or cat owners come from totally different sections of the country. One of my other discoveries included that women were anxious to share stories and wonderful pictures of their pets with me. The men shared their stories, but were quick to point out that they did not want their names mentioned in the book. For the record, on our ghost tours, the attendance is split between men and women fifty/fifty. The men ask the most questions and then pretend that they are only on the tour because their significant other made them go. But they are always the ones after the tour that tell us how much they enjoyed it.

As time went on, this book became more of a "crossover" book. What I mean by that is in order to understand ghost animals, you need to know a little about ghosts and a little about animals. So there are times, when I have included ghost information in the Appendix. When I lead a ghost tour, I always make it perfectly clear that I am not a paranormal investigator. I am not the person waiting in the cemetery hoping something will move so I can capture it on camera. Don't misunderstand, I love when there are paranormal happenings on my tours, I just do not want to be the first to discover them.

The collection of stories featured in this book include several animals species, but there are so many more out there. There are dogs, and since I am the proud "godmother" of many cats, I knew I had to include them in the book. There is even a story about a ghost horse and a lovebird!

I hope these tales are just the beginning of ghost animals becoming as "normal" or "paranormal" as other ghost stories. If you have a story you would like to share, please contact me at peggy@ghosttoursoftheouterbanks.com; I'm ready to listen!

Communicating with Animals

Many owners have very strong bonds with their animals and believe that they can read their minds. This is not far from the truth. According to Sue Erwin, an animal communicator from Fairfield, Virginia, animals can communicate with us in several ways. One of the ways a person can communicate with their animal is by sending them thoughts through an animal communicator. These thoughts can also be transmitted through images and through emotional feelings such as hate, fear, and love. Physical sensations such as headaches, stomach aches, arthritis and twinges can be sent back and forth through our animals as well. Did you ever wonder how your animal knows when you are not feeling well? Some animals can even detect cancer. Telepathic communication can be even be done with animals that have passed away.

Persons who want to try to communicate with their animals should always ask permission first. Sue said she always does this and has only been turned down once. Then when she explained to the animal what she intended to do, the animal granted permission. "Animals are very insightful and nonjudgmental," she said. "Our animals do not care what clothes we wear or how much money we have. If we take the time and effort to listen to our animals they have very important messages to share with us."

Sue described the field of animal communication in a very succinct way. "We are translators from the animal world to the people that they love. We cover many fields of communication, just like a general practitioner in the human medicine world would."

I asked Susan to describe how she decided to move from her very successful career in the corporate world to her new life as an innkeeper and animal communicator. This story began when she lost her beloved Irish Setter. She continued to grieve for her for almost two years. Then one day, she received a very interesting phone call from a friend. The friend could not wait to tell her about the experience that she just had.

"I have just been to an animal communicator," she said. The communicator said that there was a dog there that had a message for your friend. The dog wanted to thank my friend with the blonde hair for her hospitality and kindness. The dog explained that this friend was very close to St. Frances of Assisi." The communicator described the dog as a large German Shepherd. Sue was confused because she did not own a German Shepherd and could not imagine what dog this was.

Later she realized that she did rescue a stray that had been a mixed breed. But if you had to define the dog, it was a German Shepherd. Sue called her friend back and wanted to know more about what the dog had said. The dog had wanted to tell Sue goodbye and to thank her for her kindness. Now, Sue describes herself as a very analytical person, but she has always been extremely close to all kinds of animals. She has a strong belief that she has the ability to communicate with them. So she began her research and took a class with Carol Gurney, a leading expert in the field of animal communication.

She described Carol's methods as one that fit her personality and allowed her capabilities to grow. She continues to expand her skills and sincerely enjoys her communication with all types of animals.

Because the field of animal communication can bring forth a lot of skeptics, one of the first lessons that Sue had to learn was to secure verifiable information from the animals. Sue will ask very specific questions that only the person would know about their animal. For example, she will ask the pet its likes or dislikes, maybe describe a favorite food or toy or favorite location in the house. Animal communicators are told to never ask the human about the animal's personality because that may influence the communication.

All of us have the capabilities to communicate with animals. But because we do not use the skill, and society frowns upon individuals who do, the skill will atrophy. Children retain this skill for some time. This is one of the explanations why children will play with "imaginary" animal friends that are really animal spirits.

Animal communicators are there to help an animal's person in numerous ways. They can provide valuable information to that person by helping to find lost animals, correcting bad behavior, determining physical ailments, and assisting those near death to communicate to their person. They also can communicate with those animals that have passed over. Other recommendations that a communicator can make to a human is to work with a veterinarian, do additional training, experiment with Bach remedies, incorporate the healing touch into their daily routine, or suggest a change in diet.

Another animal communicator who has day to day contact with animals is Karen Douglass, the owner of All Creatures Great and Small, LLC, located in Collegeville, Pennsylvania. Karen left a lucrative career as a corporate trainer to open her own pet sitting business that includes classes in first aid and animal behavior. In several of our talks, she mentioned that she talked to animals many times and they in turn spoke to her.

I was interested in learning if certain animals were chattier than others. In her experience, dogs, especially little ones, seem to communicate the most. They might be a little afraid at first, but then after permission is granted, they really opened up. Karen feels the best way to communicate with animals is by visualizing what you would like them to do. She often used this technique when riding and competing with her horses. She would visualize what she would want them to do and then communicate it with pictures to her horse.

Karen had her own interesting story with an animal communicator. She used to ride and train at small stable in Royersford, Pennsylvania. There she had a standard bred horse named Danny that she just could not get to left lead canter. No matter how hard she tried, she was unable to get Danny to do it. One day, there was an animal communicator at the stables.

"Can you ask Danny why he will not left lead canter?" she asked the communicator. Danny, or shall we say Doctor Danny, came back with the answer. "Something is wrong with my rider's left hip," he said.

Karen thought this was interesting but totally ridiculous. "I'm fine and nothing is wrong with my hip," she scoffed.

Unfortunately, later than year, Karen had an accident that forced her to go to a chiropractor. There at the chiropractor she found out that her one leg was a quarter inch shorter than the other and her pelvis had a tilt to it. This made it difficult to position her body in the way that would enable the horse to left lead canter. Since this incident, Karen has been able to adjust her body position to be able to make the most of her and her horse's skills. She often wonders if Danny should have gone to medical school.

Like many of the people mention in the upcoming stories, I too have used an animal communicator. For fourteen years, I had a Yorkshire Terrier named Remington. My parents purchased him for me when I got divorced and moved back to New Jersey from Massachusetts. He was my constant companion and my "assistant" in the yarn shop I opened. Years later, I moved to Pennsylvania where I met my future husband. Three months before we were married, Remington suddenly died. I was devastated.

As I struggled to decide whether to get another puppy, I spoke with an animal communicator. She told me that Remington was there to help me through a difficult transition and he had now moved on to his next assignment. I have kept that in my heart for many years and share that philosophy with my friends whenever their animal passes on. I like to think of our pets as secret agents moving onto their next assignment, but sometimes they return incognito to guide us through a rough patch.

Another time I asked for the help of an animal communicator was when I was having trouble with Pixie, an adorable petite Jack Russell Terrier that I had gotten from my breeder friend. It was one of the only two girls that his favorite female had produced. He was not able to keep both girls because they both had strong personalities and would fight. So we kept the calmer of the two.

Since Pixie was so cute, we wanted to show her in confirmation. One day, my husband took her into the confirmation ring. That day she was to be examined by a male judge. When judging Jack Russells, the judge in the Jack Russell Terrier Club of America will "squeeze" or "flex" the chest to determine its flexibility as well as examine their teeth and coat. Pixie was doing fine until the judge came to her chest. All of a sudden she squealed and wiggled out of his grasp. We couldn't figure out what had happened.

From that time on, Pixie began a series of aggressive movements toward men. She would stare at them and try to incite them to look at her. When they did she would growl and snarl. She stopped going near men when any came to visit and she was terrified when she encountered them on walks.

I had no idea what to do. Finally, a friend recommended that I speak with an animal communicator whom she had recently used. At the appointed time, I called her and began a conversation. But before I could even explain the problem, she said that I had to hold on that someone was interrupting her. It is a white male dog that keeps insisting that we talk to him first. He told the communicator that he knew everything and was much more interesting than any other dog in the house.

That perfectly described my male, Scrappy. The communicator patiently told Scrappy that today was the day to speak to Pixie and that we would talk to him at another time. After complaining about some of the other dogs in the house, Scrappy agreed and wandered from the room. As the communicator returned her focus to Pixie, she began telling this story.

She said Pixie had been dropped when she was a puppy by her previous owner and it not only hurt her physically, but emotionally as well. When he dropped her, it destroyed the trust that she had in him. That distrust in men became apparent again when she was in the confirmation ring. It seemed that the judge had squeezed her chest too hard and it hurt her. What she couldn't understand was why my husband, who she absolutely adored, had let that happen.

The communicator asked Pixie what we could do to build that trust again. Pixie wanted us to begin communicating more openly with her. She wanted us to tell her when we expected male visitors and explained potential frightening experiences to her. While to this day she is more trustful of women, her distaste and distrust for men has dissipated.

Now I must admit, at the time, I was skeptical about this. So after this phone conversation, I called Pixie's breeder and asked if she had fallen or had been dropped when she was a puppy. He told me I was crazy and nothing like that had ever happened to her. I accepted that explanation. However, months later, as we were having lunch and discussing our dogs, our discussion turned to Pixie.

He let it slip that once when he had gotten frustrated with Pixie's litter, he had picked her up and thrown her across the room. Needless to say, I now have confidence and a strong belief in animal communicators. Pixie, now ten years old, has gone on to enjoy many exciting adventures and has even done some modeling for a line of doggie sweaters.

Pixie tried
animal communication
to assist her humans
in understanding her.

Do Animals Return as Ghosts?

Can animals come back as ghosts? For those individuals who are not animal lovers, there can be much controversy whether or not an animal has a spirit or a soul. But pet owners, who make their animal companions part of their family, will tell you that their animal's energy is the same as theirs. The bond and connection between owner and pet can be so strong that it can survive after death. The energy, whether brought into the present because of this bond or the energy of the animal's spirit, will enable the animal to return.

Some animal communicators, gave me a different story. According to Linda Gess, a noted animal communicator, animals are actually spirits that have already crossed over but can continue to appear on this earth. Animals are pure love and are here to teach us many things. Two of the most important are unconditional love and forgiveness. Our pets will reappear on this earth because the lessons they have to teach us have not yet been learned by us. So if they pass on before their job is completed, they will return in some way to be sure you stay on the correct path. However, once you have learned your lesson or are ready to go onto the next chapter in your life, your animal will move on to their next phase as well.

Linda also explained that animals actually choose the time when they will pass on. This explains why a perfectly healthy animal one day, will become ill and past away quickly. If it is the animal's time to pass on and they are unable to, they will ask another animal to assist them in some way. Linda said that sometimes a deer, knowing it is their time to move on, will "take the bullet" for another deer.

I asked the same question about ghost animals to Sue Erwin. She said that while she had never experienced the actual physical presence of a ghost animal, many of her clients have. They say that they have seen the fleeting image of their pet out of the corner of their eye. Numerous pet owners have said they can actually feel their presence.

One of Sue's client told the story of her ghost dog that decided to pay a return visit for the holidays. First Sue needed to verify for her client that this was the actual dog. "Tell me something about the family that you enjoyed," she asked the dog. "I loved to spend the evenings with my family watching television and eating popcorn. And I know my human did something special to remember me this holiday season."

When Sue communicated this information to the owner, tears slowly began to form in her eyes. "I hung a red bow on the tree for her," she said. "And I know it is silly, but I told her that this bow was for her." Later that day, the trash barrel in the kitchen was knocked over, but no one was near it to do the deed. The owner knew that her dog had returned to wish them a happy holiday.

Another memorable story for Sue was one about a little dachshund that had passed on. After a few weeks, the human had asked Sue to please contact her dog to see if she was alright. "Where are you right now?" Sue asked.

The dog replied, " I am here in a black velvet box with pinpoints of lights all around me."

"What are those pinpoints of light?" Sue inquired.

"They are the others that are on their way. I am in the process of getting there, I don't know where I am going, but I know it will be good," replied the little dachshund.

"It sounds beautiful," Sue said. "Please, can you share that feeling with me?" Sue said at that time she experienced the most overwhelming feeling of love. Her heart felt as if it were going to burst. It was a very wonderful and emotional experience, she recalled. "Animals," she described, "lead many lives and do not fear death. They know they are here for a short time but can choose to return to earth at any time."

Introducting the Animals!

Kelly, the Pembroke Corgi

Dee Kuhn, a long time Corgi breeder from Texas, told me that all dog owners have one. It is the one dog that you will never forget. You think about him or her every day, and many years after they are gone, tears will form in your eyes when you think of them. You compare, even though you shouldn't, your other dogs to him or her. This type of dog, according to Dee, is your "heart dog." For her, it was Kelly, her Pembroke Corgi.

Corgis originally were bred to herd cattle, but today are wonderful companions. You may have seen pictures of them with the Queen of England, walking briskly with her through the countryside. Corgis appear to have a perpetual smile on their faces because they face each day with excitement and enthusiasm. A Pembroke Corgi is known as the Corgi without a tail. They stand about ten to twelve inches tall and weigh around twenty to twenty-six pounds.

Kelly

Kelly was a magnificent example of her breed. Not only was she a confirmation stand-out but the proud recipient of multiple obedience and trailing trials. She was consistent with her training and also with her overwhelming devotion to Dee. When she died at age fifteen and one half, Dee was heartbroken. One day when Dee was feeling blue, she turned around and there was Kelly. She couldn't believe it. But, every so often, she would turn and there Kelly would be. Her presence was felt in every room in Dee's house. If Dee was in the room, Kelly's presence would be there too.

To this day, she continues to see Kelly, but she is not surprised. Her "heart dog" will never leave her.

Just as if you have one, yours will never leave you, either.

Corgis enjoy relaxing with their family.

Elmo and Lottie, the French Bulldogs

French Bulldogs or "Frenchies" are truly an international breed and have a very colorful past. It is believed that the breed began in England. These little bulldogs were actually the "runts" of a litter who traveled with the Normandy lace workers when they migrated to France. They became very popular for chasing rats and being loving companions. Because they were so cute and would bring attention to anyone who walked them, they quickly became the favorites of the "Belles De Nuit" or we would call them—prostitutes. The ladies also found that they were a quiet breed that enjoyed a quick nap in a hotel room! If you enjoy French history and antiques, you maybe able to find French postcards with scantily-clad women carrying their French Bulldogs.

These tenacious pups come in several colors, including cream, fawn, brindle, and tiger. They are approximately twelve inches in height and can weigh around twenty-six pounds. Frenchies are very happy little dogs that require a minimal amount of exercise. They adore their humans and need lots of close human contact.

Elmo

I interviewed Elmo and his owner just after he was awarded a 2008 Award of Merit at the Westminster Kennel Club Show. His owner explained that even thought he was champion, he still loves to play and is always up for a good chase. It does not make a difference to him that his "target" is a little nine-month-old white kitten ghost. His owner confided to me that she has seen this little ghost kitten scampering through the hallway. She has inquired about his story, but no one seems to know why he is there. But that does not stop him from having a good time at the "Frenchies" expense. Every day at Elmo's home in Bend, Oregon, the mischievous kitten stands at the top of the stairs and meows to attract his attention. Elmo rounds up his other Frenchie housemates and the chase begins. The kitten will take off with the dogs following close behind. Just as they are about to catch up to her, she disappears. This leaves the Frenchies frustrated, but ready to play with their paranormal friend another day.

Lottie

Another French Bulldog named Lottie was a devoted family member. She adored her family and took great pride in protecting her property. Tragically, she was killed at a young age by an automobile. Imagine the surprise of her family one day, when they looked out their front  window and saw Lottie. She was patrolling her property back and forth on the front lawn. After many years, she still can be seen on patrol, keeping her family safe from harm. What else would you expect from a kennel named "Enchant a Bull"?

Sauci, the Mini Dachshund

Many of us know the dachshund as the wiener dog. It actually means "badger dog" which the standard size Dachshund were bred to chase. The Miniature Dachshund was bred to chase rabbits. Dachshund's coats come in three varieties—smooth, long-haired, and wirehaired. Dachshunds are energetic and playful, but also can be stubborn and aggressive. They like to dig and chase small animals. But they make excellent watchdogs because, while they are small, they have a strong, loud bark.

Sauci

Sauci, the mini dachshund, enjoyed her family so much she lived to a ripe old age of seventeen and one half. She weighed approximately ten pounds and stood no more than six inches off the ground.

As you can imagine, with a dog that low to the ground, tripping over Sauci was a daily activity in her household. Sauci also liked to stick very close to her family members' feet which made the tripping problem even more pronounced.

Thirty days after Sauci passed away, every member of her family began tripping over something again. How could they all suddenly become so clumsy? When they would look around to see what they had tripped over, nothing was there. The tripping continued for thirty more days and then stopped. To this day, the family believes that Sauci came back to make sure that her family was fine before she left this earth for the final time.

Spotty, the Shetland Sheepdog

During a business trip to Reno, Nevada, I had time to do a little relaxing. So while I was sitting poolside, I got into a discussion about animals with several of the other women attending the conference. As our talk strayed to animal ghosts, I asked if anyone had had any of these experiences. One woman emphatically told me yes, that she knew her deceased dog had come to visit her on several occasions.

Spotty

Spotty was her Shetland Sheepdog. The Shetland Sheepdog is an extremely popular breed in the United States, Japan, and Great Britain. One of the first things that you will hear about the Shetland Sheepdog from breeders and from the announcers at dog shows, is that they are NOT miniature Collies. Originally used as a sheep herding dog in the 1700's in Great Britain, today's Shetland Sheepdog is used predominantly for companionship. However, they do enjoy having a job whether that is guarding the house or the bed, herding sheep or children, or performing in the agility or obedience rings. The Shetland Sheepdog stands about fourteen to fifteen inches tall and can weigh anywhere from fourteen to sixteen pounds. They can be found in several colors from the most popular tan and white, to black and white, to blue merle or even a tricolor.

In order to let Spotty the Shetland Sheepdog in and out of the house and into their fenced-in yard, Jill from California installed a doggy door. While a doggy door is very convenient, it also does make a very distinctive sound when the dog goes in and out. Spotty enjoyed this freedom and loved the ability to move back and forth at will. He also liked the fact that the doggy door lead straight into the kitchen. That access proved to be very useful and efficient when it came to suppertime. Most dog owners are truly amazed at how a dog that is sound asleep can wake up instantly and be at your side when a bag of potato chips is opened.

When Spotty passed, life was just not the same for Jill. She would be in the kitchen, but had no little companion to keep her company. One day she heard the distinctive doggy door sound. She looked over and there was no one there. Since she was concerned that another animal might be using the door, Jill went outside to looked around. No one was there. This happened several times. The door would make the sound—sometimes it even would move back and forth—but no one was there. Then one day she saw him out of the corner of her eye. There was Spotty standing by his doggy door one more time.

When Jill finished telling the story we were all in tears. Our little companions don't forget us, we just need to be aware to receive the messages that they send.

Benny, the English Setter

The English Setter has earned the nickname of the "Gentleman." They have a flat coat with what can be called "feathering" on its ends. Their coat requires significant brushing and can be a variety of speckled colors including white with black flecks, or white with tan flecks. English Setters are gun dogs and enjoy working in the field. They are athletic with a high energy level. When they are outside they love to run and work with their masters. However, when they are inside, they prefer to be "Couch Potatos."

Benny

This was so true of Benny, the English Setter from Bakersfield, California. He was a hard worker, but he also knew how to relax. His favorite chair was a leather rocking recliner in the living room. After he passed away at the age of nine, his family would often look over to see a doggy indentation in the leather rocking chair.

"But that wasn't there before," they would think. And the chair would be warm—just like when Benny had been sitting in it. The chair would then begin rocking on its own. This always happened in the evening, when it was Benny's time to relax.

Benny must have enjoyed that chair so much, he had to revisit it after he had left this world!

Boswell, the Westie

The West Highland Terrier or Westie's bright, round, white face and happy "smile" has made it a very recognizable breed. It also has landed them numerous advertising contracts including whiskey and dog food. These mischevious terriers weigh anywhere from fifteen to twenty pounds and stand about eleven inches tall. But as adorable as they are, they are very prone to allergies and skin issues. As they age, these skin conditions can become progressively worse. This will cause the Westie's coat to release a distinctive and not-so-pleasant odor.

Boswell

Boswell, the West Highland Terrier, who shared his home with several Petit Basset Griffon Vendeens (PBGBs), in Cape Cod, Massachuetts, had this affliction. The PBGBs took offense to Boswell's condition and, as some dogs will, they began to pick on Boswell. So Boswell's owners found him another home with one of their dearest friends.

A true terrier, even in his old age, Boswell enjoyed playing in his yard and chasing anything that moved. His favorite object to chase was butterflies. When he was twelve years old, Boswell passed away. But he did not stay away for long. How did his owners know? They smelled him! But the smell wasn't in the house. They would see the butterflies flying quickly away and they would be followed by Boswell's distinct smell.

Grateful Greyhounds

Greyhounds have been primarily bred for racing and lure coursing. Known for their speed, they can reach forty-five mph in less than one and a half seconds. The males can stand between twenty-nine to thirty inches tall and weigh around seventy to one hundred pounds. The females are smaller, weighing in at sixty to seventy-five pounds and standing twenty-seven to twenty-eight inches tall.

Despite the fact that they are racing dogs, they are quite gentle and bark very little. Greyhound adoption groups will tell you that greyhounds make great pets. They adapt easily to their new human pack and get along with children and other dogs, providing those dogs are not too small. They do love their humans very deeply and have a tendency to miss them greatly when they are not around.

Harrison

Harrison, an eight-year-old black brindle greyhound, had a career as a racer. When he retired, he was adopted by sixteen-year-old Amber Star Hanrahan from Woodridge, New Jersey. It was love at first sight and so deep and emotional that when she speaks of him, still today, you can just feel how much she loved him.

After only having him for short time, Harrison suffered a stoke. He then endured a thirteen day stay in the hospital. When Harrison passed away at nine years, four days old, it was a devastating time for Amber. She agonized whether or not she would ever love another dog again.

But as animal people know, sometimes it takes just the right new animal to fill the void. That void for Amber was filled thirty days later by Flossie, an eight-year-old beagle. When Amber brought her into the house, Flossie stopped right where Harrison used to sleep. All of a sudden, she began to mournfully and softly bay as only beagles can, and a warm breeze blew quickly by her and Amber. For the first time since Harrison passed away, Amber felt a sense of peace and happiness because she knew it was Harrison.

He continued to visit the house on and off for several years. To confirm that his visits were not just her imagination, many of Amber's friends also witnessed his comings and goings. But life goes on and Amber realized that she needed to say her final good bye to her great love.

She went to their favorite spot in the house and tearfully told him how much she loved him and that he would always be in her heart. But she knew she had to let his spirit go in order for them to both move on. And when she did, this ghost moved on.

Darien

Heather, who happens to be Amber's best friend since they were fourteen years old, also had a black brindle greyhound. His name was Darien. Since greyhounds are tall, she could not drive him around in her compact vehicle. So she decided she needed a bigger vehicle to transport him. Heather adored Darien and wanted to make his life as pleasant as possible, so she decided to purchase a big green van for him.

Darien loved riding in the van. He would proudly stand up in the back in order to see the sights. When he got tired, he would turn around several times and then lay down.

When he passed away from prostate cancer, Heather was devastated. But then one day as she was driving, she heard the distinctive clinking of his tags. "No, it couldn't be," she thought. But sure enough, she looked into the rear view mirror and there he was!

Every now and then, she will hear the tags. When she looks into the rear view mirror, she sees him turn around and sit down. Eventually, since she no longer needed such a large vehicle, Heather sold the van.

When she saw the purchaser several months later, the woman mentioned something very strange that had happened in the van. Several times, she heard the distinctive clinking of dog tags. When she looked in the rear view mirror, she saw a black brindle greyhound. He would turn around several times and then disappear.

Well after all, that van was really Darien's!

Lola, the Bulldog

The bulldog is the recognized symbol of the United Kingdom and known as the mascot to numerous high schools and colleges throughout the country. I personally am proud to say that I am a Drake University Bulldog! Originally, bulldogs were bred to be aggressive, tenacious, and ferocious. They had to be in order to be used for the "sport" of "bull baiting." When bull baiting became illegal in Great Britian in the 1890s, the bulldog underwent a personality transformation.

Today's bulldog is gentle with a great personality and is a favorite in the show ring. Their job is just to be a loyal and playful companion. They do require some extra grooming and daily exercise because they can be extremely sensitive to heat and cold. If you own a bulldog—don't forget to bring your earplugs, because they can SNORE!

Lola

A beautiful red and white bulldog named Lola continued to visit her mistress after she passed away. Lola was the first of many bulldogs to come from the award-winning Mystik Kennels in Juniper, Florida. She spent her days playing with her favorite toy—Mr. Squeaky Duck. After a hard day of play, she spent her evenings enjoying a snooze at the end of her mistress's bed.

Sadly, Lola passed away at the early age of three years. But she wasn't done with her daily activities. Mr. Squeaky Duck continued to squeak, when no one was touching it. In the evening, Lola's mom felt the full pressure of a fifty-five-pound bulldog at her feet. Lola continues to check up on her mistress and of course on Mr. Squeaky Duck. She wants to be sure he is not having too good a time without her.

Jazz and Boo the Boston Terriers

Boston terriers are an American original. Wearing their trademark "tuxedo," this ten- to twenty-five-pound charmer barks only when necessary. Boston Terriers are a terrier in name only and are shown in the American Kennel Club in the non-sporting category. This cuddly companion dog really enjoys human companionship and can be a perfect pet for a senior citizen.

Boston terrier owners are as passionate about their breed as their dogs are about them. After talking to several owners, their love and devotion to their breed was heartwarming to say the least. The following stories are from two Boston Terrier breeders who tell eerily similar tales.

Jazz

The first story is from Kentucky and features a father and son. Ridley was a beautiful Boston with the classic tuxedo look. After his son, Jazz, was born, he became his constant companion. When Ridley died, Jazz continued to search for him every day. He would go throughout the house and yard, but always returned to the space in the hallway where Ridley had died.

One day, Jazz's owner heard barking outside the house. She counted all her dogs to make sure everyone was present and accounted for, and they were. Afterwards, when she let her dogs outside, she heard the barking again, but this time it was coming from inside the house. Once again she counted all her dogs, no one was missing. Five days later, Jazz went to the same spot where his dad had died and did the same. It seems that the barking came from Ridley, calling to his son Jazz to come join him.

Boo-Boo

Susan from California talked about Boo-Boo, her original Boston from twenty years ago. She referred to him as her "Guardian Angel Dog." It seems that whenever one of her dogs is about to pass on, Boo Boo appears to escort the newcomer to their new home.

A couple of days before the Westminster Dog Show, Susan noticed that Boo Boo was in the kitchen. When she turned to look again, he was gone. Later that evening, one of her elderly dogs had a seizure and passed away. She said that if the dog had not passed away, she would not have been able to go to the Show. She said that she knew that Boo-Boo had wanted her and her dogs to attend this important event. So Boo Boo had once again come to do his job and escort another friend to the other side.

Boston Terrier puppies
can just melt your
heart.

A Boston
Terrier posing
for his owner's
Christmas card.
He seems to
be saying "Do
I have to do
this?"

The Boston
Terrier appears
to be wearing a
tuxedo.

Patty, the Pomeranian

It is hard to believe that this little bundle of fluff, no bigger than eleven inches and weighing no more than five pounds, is a descendant of sled dogs. The dog is named for the former Pomeranian region in central Europe which is now the northern part of Poland and eastern Germany.

Pomeranians did not start out this small, but breeders in England eventually worked it down to the size that we see today. Pomeranians have a fox-like head with a double coat. This double coat means that there is a harsh top coat with a soft coat underneath it. This keeps the dog extra warm in the winter. Pomeranians are one of the AKC's most popular breeds and they can be seen on the arms of numerous celebrities.

A Pomeranian owner knows that in that small package is a big loving heart. They also become like potato chips or chocolate chip cookies. Many owners once they have a "Pom," always want to have more. As I was writing this book, I met a wonderful little Pomeranian that was studying to be a therapy dog. More and more Pomeranians are exploring this career.

Patty

Sometimes an owner develops such a strong bond with their pet that it goes beyond animal/human companionship. Such was the story of Patty the Pomeranian and her owner, Jane. Even though Jane had numerous dogs and was a breeder of two other breeds, her relationship with Patty was remarkable. It was almost as if they could read each other's minds. So when Patty drew close to seventeen years of age and fell seriously ill, her owner realized that their time together was growing shorter.

Patty passed away silently in her sleep on Christmas Eve. That same evening, miles away, a dear friend of Jane was sleeping soundly in her bed. She woke up suddenly to see Patty walking into the room. "Patty," she exclaimed. "What are you doing here?" Patty continued to prance proudly around the room and then she disappeared.

The next morning, the friend could not wait to call Jane to tell her about the strange occurrence that had happened the night before. When she called Jane, she found her reeling from Patty's departure. When her friend began explaining the happenings of the night before, they compared times. They found the "visitation" happened after Patty had left this world.

Jane believes that Patty visited her friend because she knew her beloved owner would be too heart broken to see her one more time. But she wanted to make sure that Jane knew that she was happy and at peace.

Tony, the English Springer Spaniel

The names of the animal and the owner in this story have been changed to protect their identities. Some pets start off their lives being loved and cared for by an adoring family. Unfortunately, some animals do not have the same opportunity. They are purchased by cruel individuals who abuse them when the animals do not meet their expectations.

Tony

Tony, the English Springer Spaniel, was one of those dogs. His original owner was a horse trainer who would tie him up outside the horse barns. When Tony would bark or otherwise try to act like a dog, the owner would beat him. In fact, it became so bad, that one day the owner hit him so hard, it broke Tony's jaw.

Joan was a true animal lover. She assisted in training the horses and would see Tony every day. When she saw what was happening to him, it made her physically ill. "How could anyone be that cruel to such a beautiful animal?" she thought.

One day, Joan decided that she could not watch this happen anymore. She returned to the barn late one evening to find Tony. When she did, she untied Tony and took him home with her. The next day, she watched as the original owner screamed and yelled about his dog that had run away. She commiserated with him and agreed that the dog had run away.

Basically, now in a witness protection program,

Tony's life changed dramatically. He lived with Joan in a small row home in Philadelphia. There he had all the amenities a dog would want. There were plush beds, great food, and lots of toys. But the most important change was now Tony was loved and adored. Since he was her only dog, Joan showered him with love and affection. At least once a month, he would ride with Joan to her vacation home in the Poconos enjoying the countryside and fresh air. Tony lived a wonderful life for many years. Sadly he became ill very suddenly and passed away without any warning.

Joan was distraught. She wanted a chance to make things right for Tony. She tortured herself with questions on what she could have done differently. These feelings prevented her from wanting another dog. In fact, she swore to herself she would never get another dog again.

Then one day, Joan was on her way to work. Since she worked with horses, she needed to be at the barns by 5 am. So that morning, she was up and on the road by 4 am. It was a particularly foggy and rainy morning, making it very difficult to navigate the roads. All of a sudden, she spotted something along the road. "What was it?" she asked. As she came closer to the object, she decided to pull over to the side to see what it was. She couldn't believe her eyes. There was an English Springer Spaniel, exactly like Tony.

Joan opened the car door and urged the dog to jump it. He quickly did so and assumed his position in the passenger's seat, just as Tony used to do. To this day, Joan swears that the dog she found by the side of the road was her same dog that had returned to her.

Driving Miss Daisy Crazy, the Miniature Poodle

Did you know that the Poodle may not have originated in France? Because Poodles are one of the oldest breeds, there are rumors that the dogs originated in Russia or even Germany. But French breeders have been credited for creating the three sizes of Poodle—Standard, Miniature, and Toy. While some may scoff at the Poodle's show clip, they are in reality working dogs. They were traditionally used as retrievers and spent a great deal of time in cold water.

Today, they also are excellent performers in the obedience and agility rings. The majority of us however see the "people-pleasing" Poodles in the Confirmation Ring.

Angelo

Driving Miss Daisy Crazy, or as he is better known, Angelo, was the top winning Miniature Poodle in 2007. As I spoke with his owner at the Westminster Kennel Club Show, his little black face and piercing black eyes just radiated the mischievous and old soul that his owner believes he is. Even though Angelo was from a good litter, he was to be his owner's "Starter Mini." A "Starter

Dog" is the one where you learn all your mistakes. Since Angelo's owner was a dog show novice, the breeder felt that he would be a perfect Poodle for her. She could make all her mistakes with him before she really started showing Poodles.

But Angelo had other ideas. Once the leash was attached, Angelo, at eight weeks old, just took over. He seemed to know how to do everything that was required of him in the show ring. He knew how to bait, stand, stick, you name it in the dog show world, and he did it. His show career, with a novice at the end of the leash, has been wildly successful. His owner is convinced that he is a very old soul, a champion who has done it all before and is back here to do it once again.

When she finished telling the story, I looked Angelo over one more time. And you know, I think he winked at me!

Roxie, the Rhodesian Ridgeback

The "Lion Dog" or Rhodesian Ridgeback today is known to be a devoted and loyal member of the family. He is not the hunting dog that he was originally bred to be. In the past the Ridgeback, with other pack members, would keep lions "at bay" until the hunter arrived. There are numerous stories about the loyalty to their family demonstrated by the Rhodesian Ridgebacks. Their numerous fans are usually experienced dog owners who understand that training a Ridgeback needs a firm but fair hand. Their name is derived from the ridge of hair along its back that grows in the opposite direction.

Roxie

Roxie, the Rhodesian Ridgeback, was the foundation bitch of her Reddington, Connecticut kennel. Both Roxie and her granddaughter Riva were powerful, muscular, loyal, and affectionate bitches that stood twenty-seven inches tall and weighed around eighty-five pounds. The only difference was their noses. Roxie had a black nose and Riva, a liver-colored one.

One day after Roxie had passed, her owner turned to look at Riva. She was sitting in the exact same spot where Roxie used to relax. When Riva picked up her head and looked at her owner, there was no mistaking it—her nose was black.

"No, it couldn't be," her owner exclaimed.

As you can imagine, she thought she was going crazy. So she closed her eyes, shook her head, and looked again. Riva was looking at her slyly with her liver-colored nose. Was it the light or maybe some dirt? No, Roxie's owner firmly believes that her foundation bitch had come back one more time to be sure Riva was up to the task.

The Ridgeback has a line of hair that stands straight up down the middle of their back.

Spectre's Belgian Sheepdogs

Long Island, New York, is home to Spectre's Belgian Sheepdogs and two very good friends—Peggy and Terri. They met over fourteen years ago, when Peggy asked Terri to train her daughter's Dalmatian.

When Terri arrived at Peggy's house, she spotted some adorable puppies on her front lawn. "What are they?" Terri exclaimed. "They are so adorable!" Eighteen months later, Terri got her first Spectre's Belgian Sheepdog puppy. It has forever linked the two friends in their love for their dogs and the paranormal experiences that they share with them.

When I first met them, they were quick to tell me *Spectre* means *ghost* and they had numerous stories to share that proved the kennel was worthy of that name.

While I was researching the breed to give the reader a picture of these wonderful dogs, I found that they had several names. There are four breed varieties—the Groenendal, the Laekeknois, the Tervuren, and the Malinois. In some areas, the varieties are recognized as one breed. In the United States, the American Kennel Club recognizes the Groenedael as the Belgian Sheepdog. All four varieties have similar sizes and temperament. The major differences are their coats and minor physical characteristics. Normally, the dogs weigh between sixty-five and seventy-five pounds and stand twenty-four to twenty-six inches tall.

I found the personality traits of the dogs extremely interesting and a perfect compliment to the ghost stories that you will read. Belgian Sheepdogs form extremely close relationship bonds with their humans. They love being with them so much that they have a tendency to become a one-person dog. Belgian Sheepdogs love to work. In reality, they need to work to keep intellectually and physically stimulated. They can be trained to do agility, dog tricks, herding, and even picking up dirty laundry! They are very intelligent dogs that are alert to all that is going on around them.

Ghost

The Spectre legend begins with Summit's Ghost of Gallahad. Ghost was a "waiter." Not the kind that brings you food, but the dog that is always there to greet you when you come home. Ghost was the one that somehow knew that not every member of the family was in the house. So he always would position himself in front of a window or a door to wait.

Today, even in death, Ghost is the one that will wait for the other dogs to cross over. When he is spotted, both Peggy and Terri know that they will be losing a member of their doggy family soon. In fact, when one of their dogs become ill, one of the first questions they will ask each other is, "Are you seeing anybody?"

When Ghost was fifteen years old, he became extremely ill. Peggy knew the time had come to say goodbye to her beloved friend. To make the transition easier for him, arrangements were made to have the veterinarian come to the house. Also in the house,

Peggy had a three-week-old litter of puppies which she kept in the kitchen. Ghost was the sire or daddy to this litter. When the vet arrived to help Ghost pass into the afterlife, all of the puppies began to howl. The puppies continued to howl until the vet had completed his job and Ghost was gone. All at once, all the puppies stopped howling.

Later that evening, Peggy had a dream about Ghost where he was beautiful and whole. "This was a sign," she said. Ghost wanted her to know that he was okay, but would be there whenever she needed him.

Spirit was one of those howling puppies. Because he was three weeks old when his father passed, he never spent any time with him. But one day, when Spirit was a littler older, he had a reunion with his father. Peggy was in the living room watching television when a commercial came on with some very unusual music. She said she got a very funny feeling and could feel a definite presence. Spirit quickly woke up from a

CH Summits Ghost of Galahad
owned by Peggy Koller.

sound sleep, stood up, walked over to where Ghost had his dinner every evening and sat there for ten minutes. He moved his head the way dogs do when they are trying to understand something. Then, just as quickly, Spirit got up and returned to his previous position. He immediately fell back asleep. Peggy believes that Ghost returned to visit his son.

Several years later in mid-August, Terri came to the Peggy's house to deliver some devastating news about her beloved Belgian Bella. Seven-year-old Bella had just been diagnosed with cancer. As she opened the gate to Peggy's yard, she saw a beautiful dog on the front lawn, in perfect show stance looking straight ahead. But the most unique thing about the dog was his fur. It was blowing about, just as if it was in a strong wind. What had caused this? There was not even a breeze that day.

When Terri turned around again, the dog was gone. She did not mention it to Peggy—what would she think? But three nights later, she saw the same dog again, just the head. The eyes were so distinctive, she could not get them out of her mind. And what was even stranger was that the Belgian Sheepdog that Terri has tattooed on her shoulder was the same dog.

Finally, Terri just had to tell Peggy—it was just too strange. When she heard the story, Peggy smiled. "It's Ghost," she said. "Wind was always Ghosty's friend—whenever it was windy and I showed him, he did well." Ghost, the "waiter" was waiting for Bella, who died one month later.

Bella

Bella too comes back. Terri is the owner of Bow Wow Boulevard, Grooming and Smart Dog Training. Terri credits Bella for being the reason that she opened the business and feels her presence on a day-to-day basis there.

One day, a customer was having a discussion with Terri about dogs and the afterlife. Since this might be a touchy subject with some people, he had always kept his thoughts to himself. But that day he said to Terri, "You do know that there is a dog sitting right behind you. She has been watching everything that you have been doing. She is close enough to almost touch you." Terri knew that this had to be Bella who had passed away five months after Terri had opened the shop.

The day that Peggy, Terri, and her daughter picked up Bella's ashes, it was a devastating day, as anyone who has ever loved an animal knows. But as they were sharing their grief, they all heard a little girl's voice calling out softly, "Bella." Once again, no one wanted to admit they heard it, but later as they discussed the day, all three confirmed hearing that voice.

Years later, Terri visited a medium who told her that Bella's job now is to look after a little girl with blonde hair. It is possible that the little girl they are describing is a friend's daughter who matches the description and passed away at the young age of fourteen. Bella adored children and her love for them is carried on in the afterlife.

And now, her love for children has been passed on to her daughter—Echo Bella. Echo Bella loves children and is now studying to be a therapy dog. Her area of concentration will be children. In fact, with all the people and other animals at the Westminster Kennel Club Show, Echo Bella sat contentedly in the aisle, letting children hug and lay all over her. It was an amazing sight!

Ghost waiting for his owner to come home.

Cortez

When Cortez, one of Terri's Belgians, was nine years old, he was diagnosed with lymphoma. While it was not a true diagnosis, he had to begin an aggressive treatment of chemotherapy. Cortez was in really bad shape as Peggy and Terri took him to the animal center for his treatments. One day, as Peggy and Terri left him at the facility for his treatment, they both were very concerned because he was so sick, he could hardly walk. While they were waiting, they decided to get a bite to eat at the diner. So they parked their van and went inside. About a half hour later, both of them head barking. They casually looked around, but there was no dog in sight. Thinking, as people often do, that she was imagining things, Terri asked Peggy if she heard the barking. "I heard it too," she said.

For some reason, they looked over at the van and saw Cortez inside. After the Cortez sighting, Peggy began to feel very ill. About forty-five minutes later, Peggy suddenly felt much better. When they returned to the vet's office to pick up Cortez, the somber vet says, "I have never had one come back on the table."

"What are you talking about?" asked a now-hysterical Terri. The vet then explained that Cortez had died on the table—at the same time he was spotted in the van.

But Cortez had decided that it was not his time to go—just yet. He revived on the table and was actually able to walk out of the operating room into the arms of his tearful owner. Terri and Peggy could not believe that the dog they had brought in, was now walking into the van!

Cortez eventually succumbed to his lymphoma, but he still likes to pay Terri a visit on occasion.

One of my favorite sayings that I gathered as I was writing this book, I acquired from Terri. She calls them, "Postcards from Heaven." It is those little things that prove to us our animals are thinking about us and want to send us a little message. They often come when we are experiencing moments of sadness, loss, or loneliness.

For example, Terri was feeling exceptionally sad one day and decided to watch the movie, *GI Jane*. As she was watching the movies all of a sudden she had to smile. GI Jane's best friend's name was Cortez.

Another time when Terri was feeling melancholy, she decided to do some cleaning. As she was looking through a trunk, she found buried in the bottom puppy pictures of Cortez. How can you not smile!

Bella

Solis was Bella's full sister and actually one of the puppies that Terri had first seen on the Peggy's lawn all those years ago. When she died, Peggy and Terri went to pick up her ashes. As they often do during times of sadness and loss, they made their way to a Starbucks for a cup of coffee.

For some reason, Terri looked up into the sky. "Look at that!" she gasped. Flying above the shop was a small biplane flying a banner that said simply "Bella." She had sent along another heavenly "Postcard" to comfort her mistress.

Aurora

Remember the time when the paper that came out of a computer's printer was one long stream? Well, Aurora, one of Ghost's friends, certainly did. Aurora loved to pull the paper out and drag it all over the house—much like puppies love to drag toilet paper.

When she was ten years old, she passed away from cancer. But her love for dragging the paper did not die with her.

One day, Peggy's mom came home and found the computer paper all over the house. It had Aurora's tell-tale teeth marks on it, but there was no other dog present to claim responsibility.

Katie

There are times when some dogs become almost obsessed with a particular toy. They will play with it for hours and prevent any other dog from taking it away. Such was the case of Katie, another Belgian Sheepdog who loved her squeaky baby dinosaur toy.

Terry and her beloved Cortez.

When she passed away, the toy was put away, out of sight, behind the television. It was just too hard for her owners to look at it. They had quite the experience when the toy kept showing up in different rooms in the house. Every day for two weeks, the baby dinosaur toy moved and never to the same spot. No other dogs or humans have claimed responsibility for the toy's strange behavior.

Maybe Katie wanted to take the toy with her, but just could not figure out how to do it!

Leroy, the Doberman

The Big Red Machine, that is what the Chief of Police in Lower Frederick Township, Pennsylvania used to describe Leroy, the red Doberman. The Doberman Pinscher is a very recognizable breed that was commonly used as a police or guard dog. While the breed may have had some bad publicity years ago, today the breed is known for it energy and love that they shower on their families.

Leroy began his life as a rescue dog. He was found emaciated, wandering along a creek. His foster parents were a three-year-old girl and her mother. It was from this experience that Leroy began his love affair with the ladies. Many people were frightened by the looks of this big barrel-chested boy. But when a lady came on the scene, Leroy was putty in her hands. Whenever his parents gave a party, he would seek out the single females and assume the proprietary position at their feet for the entire evening.

Leroy was also a home body, never really wanting to leave his home, a thirteen-acre farm in Pennsylvania. But his family had other ideas. They like to spend a week each year at the Outer Banks in North Carolina. Leroy hated leaving the farm and expressed his displeasure by refusing to eat and barking at the seagulls in his temporary home.

Then one summer, things changed. Leroy decided that the beach was not so bad after all. He would joyfully run to the ocean the moment he got out of the van and give his parents a great big smile.

As he got older, it became more and more difficult to transport Leroy to the beach because of his arthritis. Eventually, his owner made a ramp for him to climb into the van. But he always perked up once he hit that sandy beach and scampered into those beautiful waters.

When he got to the house, he couldn't make it up the stairs anymore. So his family bought him a big blue bed and placed it at the base of the stairs. There he lounged the days away.

His housemates, Chippy, Scrappy, and Indy, the Jack Russells would come and visit or sometimes just plain annoy him. But how bad could things be at the beach? His family would always take a picture of him every time they took him to the beach. They believed that if they continued to take that picture, he would continue to live on and on.

But one day, within two hours of returning from the beach to his beloved farm in Pennsylvania, Leroy had a stroke. The next day, he went out into the yard and laid down in the same spot where another beloved Doberman had been buried. His parents knew that it was a sign. Later that week, they made the tough decision to help him pass.

Several months later, the family returned to the beach. It was a sad occasion because one of their members was not there.

When they opened the garage door, Chippy, Scrappy, and Indy raced over to Leroy's bed. They were barking and jumping, showing more joy than they had in months. As their owners looked on, they saw that the bed had a fresh indentation in it. It was just the size of their big Doberman.

It seems their beloved friend was still enjoying his favorite spot afterall.

Leroy smiling on the beach
in the Outer Banks.

Casey, the Golden and Rush, the Border Collie

If you talk to a skeptic about ghost animals, I am sure that they would provide you with a logical explanation. They will say, "Two dogs of the same breed have similar characteristics and that is why their behaviors are eerily similar." But the owners of Casey and Rush from Connecticut were unable to use this explanation.

Casey was a golden retriever mix, with the personality traits of a Golden Retriever. He was calm, alert, easy to train, and good with children. He never snapped at a family member and would sooner lick an intruder than bite them. Casey was a well-loved dog and his family was devastated when he died at the early age of two. Since Casey was their "heart dog," the family agonized over whether to even get another dog. How could anyone ever compare?

But after nine months without a dog, they finally decided to adopt Rush, the Border Collie. Now Border Collies are quite a different breed. They have a strong work ethic because they have been bred to herd sheep. While they are affectionate, they need to work. If you do not provide an activity for them such as agility or obedience training they will find a job to do. That can be herding adults or children.

Rush did not exhibit any of those traits; in fact, his traits were identical to Casey's. Even the expression in his eyes down to the way he moved was Casey's. To this day, the family believes that their beloved Casey has come back to them, but in a different package.

A Border collie mix puppy.

A typical Golden Retriever enjoying his yard.

Molly- A Golden on the Move

Molly was the typical adorable Golden Retriever. Born in northeastern Pennsylvania, she was the runt of her litter. Her coloring was a little darker than the typical light golden color, but she was beautiful in the eyes of her new owners. They purchased her at eight weeks of age and brought her home to begin her new life.

She enjoyed all the typical activities of a Golden— playing with the children, running, enjoying a good game of catch and of course being petted. Goldens are an especially affectionate breed and thrive on the love that their families are willing to shower on them.

Molly especially loved the attention of her "grand-father." Whenever he would come to visit, she would follow him everywhere, demanding in her special way, for him to pet her. How could he resist? They developed a strong and lasting bond that lasted beyond life.

After all this playing and petting, Molly often-times decided that she needed a nap. Her favorite location would be on one of the little girls' bed. The bed had a little squeaky sound to it. When there was pressure put on it—whether it occurred by a little girl sitting on it or a Golden laying down for a nap—the squeaky sound could be heard even in the next room.

As time went on, Molly became a mom with a lit-ter of six puppies. She took excellent care of them, but she still needed her nap, and of course her love and affection. Tragedy struck when Molly was diagnosed with cancer at the age of six. She passed away six weeks before her beloved "grandfather" also passed away from cancer.

Now, this might have been enough of a coincidence, but the story continues. Years later, the family moved out of their home to another one several towns away. One evening, the little girl, now grown up and away from home, left her bedroom and her squeaky bed unoccupied. As the house settled into the silence of late night, there was the distinctive sound of Molly settling down into her favorite spot for a nap.

Could this be possible? Could a ghost animal follow their beloved family to a location where they had never been before? On our tours, people often tell us that they have moved into a new home and believe it is occupied by a ghost. What we have learned is that there can be numerous explanations for this. First, where is the house built? Is it above a burial ground or the site of a Revolutionary War battle? Ghosts can attach themselves to a particular person or a specific location. So maybe the new home is intruding on their territory and they are going to make their displeasure known. Another question that we ask is if anyone in the family likes to visit yard sales or flea markets? If they do sometimes spirits like to travel in mirrors, chairs, and dolls.

It is possible that Molly was very attached to her bed and traveled with it to her family's new home? Or she could have just wanted to visit them and her bed one more time?

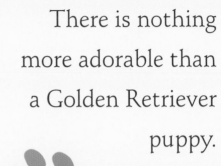

There is nothing
more adorable than
a Golden Retriever
puppy.

Dig Dog

Manteo, North Carolina, is a quaint town filled with historic buildings along a beautiful waterfront. It has numerous ghosts according to the Ghost Tours of the Outer Banks, including the famous animal legend of the White Doe and Hatteras Jack the albino dolphin. (You will read about the doe and dolphin in a later chapter.)

But Manteo also has domestic animal ghost stories including the one about Dig Dog, a Collie-Shepherd mix. He was owned by Carol who works at the Tranquil Inn, another haunted Manteo location. Dig Dog loved to lay at the bottom of the steps of his two-story home. For years, Carol and her husband tried to break him of this dangerous habit, but he "gave them the paw" and laid there every day for twelve years. One day after he died, Carol was walking down the stairs. Right before she got to the bottom, she suddenly stopped and almost fell over—you know who! Dig Dog was laying there in his favorite spot. He still was admonished, just as he always was, even if he was there just in spirit.

After losing Dig Dog, Carol was not sure whether she wanted another dog ever again. Throughout the next year, many dear friends made good-natured attempts to entice her to buy or adopt a new puppy, but she steadfastly refused.

Annoyed with these attempts she said to her husband, "We are not going to get another dog unless one comes knocking at our door."

The next day there was a knock on the door and there stood her neighbor. In her arms was a new puppy that she had just rescued. Carol's new dog had just arrived and now lives happily ever after on the Outer Banks.

Spanky, the Shepherd-Collie Mix

Spanky the Shepherd-Collie mix was Karen Douglass' soul mate. This was quite a turn of events, because in the beginning she could not stand him. He was an absolute monster. A typical day for him was crashing through doors, terrorizing the neighborhood, and always finding a way to get into trouble. He even failed puppy school three times.

Then one day, that light bulb in his doggy brain just went off and Spanky had a total turn around. He began to love training and he excelled at it. Whenever he saw that special lead that signified training time, he became excited. Spanky also had quite a vocabulary. He was able to annunciate ten to fifteen sounds and would use them to create a cohesive sentence. His love of training continued to the day he died at the age of seventeen.

After he passed, Karen was unable to get another dog for almost four years. She would often hear Spanky barking and "talking" the way he used to do. But of course, she believed that she just imagined him "talking" because she missed him so much.

Then one day Sharon, who works in the offices of Karen's business, All Creatures Great and Small, mentioned to her that she heard a dog barking. "It can't be one of yours," she commented. "Your dogs are small and they do not have that deep of bark. This dog speaks in several octaves; just like she was talking and it always comes from the garage door."

Karen then knew for sure that it was Spanky. You see, the garage door was where they would always let Spanky out. Today he still guards the house and let's Karen know that he is there.

Remington, the Yorkshire Terrier

My own ghost dog experience involves my Yorkshire Terrier, Remington. A six-pound bundle of energy, Remington was my baby. He lived with me in New Jersey and then moved on with me to Pennsylvania. His numerous jobs included: greeting customers in my yarn shop in Rutherford, New Jersey, being sure the streets were clean from debris using his little beard, and evaluating and critiquing my boyfriends. In fact, if he did not like a particular man, he would express his displeasure by lifting his leg on his shoe. The embarrassing part was the man was wearing it at the time.

Remington never met a meal he did not like and had learned that the stealth method of food begging produced the best results. Whenever a big meal was served at Thanksgiving or Christmas, he would lay quietly underneath the table. Sooner or later, he knew something would hit the floor. Sometimes, it was just a small morsel. But other times, like the time an entire sausage hit the floor, he hit pay dirt.

Remington was famous for his numerous outfits, even though I swore I would never do that. One time during a snowstorm, I put so much clothing on him,

66

he was unable to move, let alone lift his leg. He also had a sense of rhythm and loved to do his clockwise "Happy Dance." The "Happy Dance" was reserved for when he received a particularly delicious tidbit of food.

After fourteen years of love and devotion, Remington suddenly passed away. The grief I felt was overwhelming. Every night, I tried so hard to dream about him, so that somehow I would know he was okay. But nothing ever materialized.

That fall, a new puppy, Chatka Chip, the Jack Russell, entered my life. Chippy was as different from Remington as you could get. They had absolutely no common traits or behaviors. She was the ultimate handful and exhausted me every day.

As we prepared that year to celebrate Thanksgiving, it is our family tradition that everyone, including our dogs, enjoy the feast. As I went to put down her first Thanksgiving meal, Chippy stopped and did the "Happy Dance." We all stood there shocked. Tearily my mom said, "Remington is wishing us a Happy Thanksgiving."

Chippy never did the "Happy Dance" again.

A Tale from a Pet Cemetery

The following story is not a horror tale that would be featured in movie theatres. But it is set in a pet cemetery in Fogelsburg, Pennslyvania, which is located off Route 78. Lois, who worked at the cemetery for two years, told me the story of a St. Bernard that would wander the property. He was spotted by numerous workers as he moved about the cemetery every evening. He was hard to miss because St. Bernards are one of the largest breeds. Even though they are a large breed, they are friendly, love children, and are very gentle. They love to please their owners, but disipline must be learned at an early age, because they can be a handful.

St. Bernards got their name from the traveler's hospice located on the dangerous St. Bernard Pass in the Western Alps. This hospice was operated by monks who kept the dogs for companions and for help in rescuing travelers in trouble. Contrary to popular belief, St. Bernards did not wear barrels with brandy or some other type of alcohol around their necks. This is a popular myth started by a painting by John Emms.

The St. Bernard of the Cemetery did not do anything unusual or scary admitted Lois. I asked if he had experienced a tragic death. She said that no, he had died of old age. He also had been around the cemetery for a long time and was a known entity. He was an imposing sight in the evening because of his size and because he would just materialize and begin his rounds. The workers became used to him, although he would cause a quite a stir to a newcomer to the cemetery.

Since his walk would begin and end at approximately the same time every day, the workers speculate that it was the usual time his owners would normally take him on his daily walk. He is continuing the routine in the afterlife.

Violet, the Yorky- Still Making a Fashion Statement

Yorky owners are a different breed. They may swear that they will never dress up their dogs, but sometimes an outfit is just too cute to pass up. The Yorkies, while they may protest at first, really like to, shall we say, "Put on the Dog."

This is a short tale about a Yorky named Violet. It not only involves fashion, but another favorite hobby of mine—knitting.

Lisa was Violet's owner. She worked at a newspaper in Washington, D.C., but split her living time between both D.C. and Los Angeles. Lisa had several dogs, but Violet, the Yorky, was her oldest. Her bicoastal companion was special and Lisa adored her.

Over the years, Lisa became friendly with a woman who worked at the same newspaper she did. She greatly admired her friend because she had a hobby she could not master. Her friend was an expert knitter. But Lisa and her friend shared another common bond. They both were extremely devoted to their animals. As the fates would have it, both Violet and her friend's cat became very ill at the same time. The two friends would support each other as they went

through the agony of watching their beloved companions fade away. One evening as they were talking,
Lisa asked her friend to knit her a felted purse. The
money for the purse they decided would be donated
to an animal shelter. Her friend quickly knitted up
the bag. It was beautiful and done in stripes of purple,
red, and turquoise with a small stripe of violet to
represent the little Yorky. The bag, which was sent
to Los Angeles, never reached Lisa.

Violet quietly passed away one evening. Her
friend, who felt terrible about both Violet and the
missing bag, told Lisa that she would knit her another
bag. She planned to make it just like the first. Hope-
fully, this bag would get there to lift Lisa's spirits. But,
unfortunately, as her friend checked her yarn "stash,"
she could not find the violet yarn needed to make
the bag. She also learned that the yarn she originally
used was now discontinued. She was disappointed
to say the least.

Right before she planned to get started, she went
back to the same knitting basket again. She had
checked that basket over and over for the yarn the day
before. To her amazement, there in the bottom was
a small ball of violet yarn. Both Lisa and her friend
believe that it was just Violet's way of sending her
love one more time.

A Horse is a Horse, Unless It's a Ghost

Branchville, New Jersey, is a beautiful little community located in northern Sussex County. It is only on half mile in size and has only 845 residents, but it has survived two catastrophes—a fire in 1882 and a flood in 1955. So it is not surprising that Branchville has it share of ghosts. Who would have thought that one of the ghosts was a horse?

Toby

Toby was a rescue horse whose owners had previously abused him. He came to live on a farm in Branchville with a woman named Jo who had saved him from his horrible situation. Once Toby settled into his new home, Jo's goal was to have him live out the remaining years of his life in comfort and with the knowledge that he was loved. So Jo and her daughter took extra special care of him. Maybe it was extra carrots on Tuesday and a longer brushing on Wednesday, but no matter how busy they were, they made it their business to love and care for him.

Toby became a fixture at the farm. His daily routine was to stand with his head out of the barn door and watch the world go by. He would then hold court with his friends, both human and animal. His best friends were several goats that lived in the barn with him.

After he passed away, Toby would return to the place he loved the best. Jo and her daughter would find him sticking his head out of the barn door. There were times during the day, when the goats would stop eating. They would pick up their heads and then run over to the barn door. They would then stare up at the barn door, the same way they did when Toby was alive. This continued for about three years. When Jo's daughter left the farm for college, Toby never reappeared again.

Lodi- It is Not Just for Gangsters

Over the past several years, the town of Lodi, New Jersey, became famous for the television show that featured mobsters. But Lodi also has some chilling ghost animal tales that still give me the creeps, even though they happened so many years ago.

This is a story that has been passed down for generations in my family. In fact, my grandmother, or "Babci" (grandmother in Polish), was one of the reasons I have such an interest in the paranormal. This story is set in the 1940s and features two cemeteries located off River Road in Lodi. The cemetery where this story takes place is called Lodi Cemetery. They are separated by a road with sidewalks on both sides. There are significant tree canopies there and a very chilling breeze blows through the area. The atmosphere feels "old." Even in the forties, each cemetery was surrounded by a chain link fence to keep out vandals. It certainly does not feel menacing in the daytime, but night is a different story.

My grandmother worked at one of the local mills on the late shift. Since she was getting off around one in the morning each day, she would take a short cut to her home. That short cut took her on the sidewalks between the two cemeteries.

Cemetery Dog

One evening, as she was hurrying home, she heard a strange noise coming from the cemetery. She turned to see what it was and saw a large dog, growling and snapping on the other side of the cemetery fence. She froze in terror. The dog uttered a horrible snarl and charged the fence. The second it hit the fence with a loud crash, the dog evaporated into thin air. Needless to say it was the last time Caroline ever took that short cut again.

Ghost Dogs

"Babci" was not the only one who had an animal ghost story. My mother, Wanda, told the story of a beautiful Victorian home that used to be located at the end of their street. Now, in those days, there was quite a distance between houses, but rumors still got around pretty quickly. It seems that no one ever lived in that house for longer than one day.

Why? It is said that the house, which had a large staircase in the middle, was visited at the stroke of midnight by three large, black ghost dogs. The dogs would run up and down the staircase barking and growling.

When a human appeared to see what was happening, the ghost dogs would disappear. However, as soon as they went back to bed, the dogs would start up again. It became a legend in their neighborhood, but as much as people would try to live down the legend, they never could. Since no one could ever live in the house, it was eventually destroyed. One beautiful Saturday afternoon, when I was researching stories for this book, my mom and I decided to drive to the neighborhood where this house was located. Today an apartment complex sits on the site where the Victorian home once stood. We stopped to talk to several of the residents, just to satisfy our curiosity. They told us they can still hear dogs barking and growling at the stroke of midnight.

The strange thing is, there are no dogs allowed in the apartment complex and there are no dogs that can emit this strange type of bark in the area.

Coco, A True Life Saver

You never know when you will encounter a good ghost story or an even better friend. My friend, Cecile Charlton, told me this story one day when we were taking a weekend break in Cape May, New Jersey. Since I can not tell it as well as she can, I asked her to write about it for this book. This is the story in her own words.

South Jersey is well known as a favorite vacation spot for many people who live in suburban Philadelphia. It is not uncommon for families to own vacation homes that are passed down from one generation to the next. That was the case with the large Arts and Craft style home on Aster Avenue in Wildwood Crest. The home was originally bought by the family matriarch during World War II, and on her death it passed onto her son and his family.

During the 1960s and 1970s, the young family would spend the summers there with their cat, Freddie, and their dog, Coco. The father would work in Philadelphia during the week and join his family at the Shore on weekends. It was a much simpler time; the only phone available to them was the pay phone at the corner store. The two children and their mother would spend hours on the beach. The evenings were spent in the back yard playing with their dog and their friends or walking on the board-walk. Each year in August the weather would begin to change from hot but beautiful, bright sunny skies to cooler evenings. This would mark the beginning of evenings spent in the house as a few Nor'easters or hurricanes would come through. The weather would interrupt electrical service to the island and plunge the area into an eerie, quite darkness. The only warn-ing that these weather conditions were approaching was heard over the radio. Television reception was impossible at the Shore in those days either with rabbit ears or even a roof antenna.

One night in mid-August, 1967, a major storm was approaching. Tree branches were scratching the house; rain was pounding into the lawn making small rivers and ponds in the street where the drains were backed up from the high tide overflowed. There was a "pop" and the lights went out. The mother brought out the hurricane lamps and a game of "Crazy Eights" continued.

The cat was sitting on the window sill in the So-larium hissing at the leaves hitting screen. The family dog, Coco a sixty-five-pound German Sheppard mix, a fearless dog that adored her family and despised strangers, was on alert. One minute she would be lying on the floor with one of the children napping on her back, and the next, she was barking a deep, warning bark at strangers walking on the sidewalk. She was a fearless protector of kids and was known to snap at fathers who yelled at their children. Dur-ing a severe storm, this strong, sometimes scary dog, could be found hiding in one of the closets on the second floor, buried under littered clothing, terrified of the thunder.

The family was used to this weather, and Coco's disappearing act, having summered there for years. They went to bedroom, but no amount of effort or food used as a bribe worked in dislodging Coco from the closet. The door was left open, so that when the storm ebbed, she could leave and find her way to her favorite sleeping spot, an old beach blanket that she had worked into perfect softness. She slept between the doors of the children's rooms. She had placed the old blanket there herself, the family believed, so that she would not show any favoritism. Over the years, she would sleep there until the last child woke and made their way downstairs.

So it was particularly odd when, in the middle of the night, Coco became agitated and started running around the first floor of the house barking. She never did this. Coco stood with her front paws on the bottom step and barked up to the sleeping family. Only the mother awoke, so she charged up the steps and barked into each child's room. Once everyone was awake, she raced down the stairs, and looking up at the three of them and insisted everyone follow her. She ran into the living room, not used much, on the north side of the house. Once she had everyone in the room, she sat.

The mother stooped to pet Coco and asked, "What is it girl, what is wrong?" With that, one of the beach trees on the south side of the house fell onto the second floor, destroying two of the three bedrooms. The ground had been saturated by the rain and the tree was rotting, having been hit by lightning years ago. Had they stayed in their rooms, the two children would have been gravely injured or even killed.

Coco was always a beloved pet, but after her keen sense of hearing and doggy intuition saved the family, she was treated like a queen—she wanted for nothing. As she got older, she favored the daughter's soft bed to the hardness of the old blanket on the floor and would stick her cold nose under the covers and hit her feet, making her giggle.

When Coco died four years later, at the grand old age of eighteen, he was put to rest in a favorite part of the garden, next to the daughter's favorite hydrangea.

In 1998, the daughter took over the Wildwood Crest house with her two sons. The house needed some work and weekends during the spring and early summer were spent scraping wallpaper, sanding the hardwood floors, painting and cleaning. Plumbing and wiring were updated and the kitchen was given a boost into the twenty-first century. The house now had a telephone landline, Internet connection, cable television, smoke detectors, and three different cell phones in the house. But it did not have a dog.

One weekend during the spring, the daughter was awoken by the sound of a neighbor's dog barking. She got up and went to the window to see where the noise was coming from, but it had stopped. It was not that she minded a neighbor's dog outside on a beautiful night, but it was three o'clock in the morning. She went back to bed and heard it again; she did not want to close her windows, but there was a long list of chores that needed to be completed the following day.

Once again the dog began its deep barking, but this time it sounded like it was coming from the other direction. Curious, she went to the other side of the house, into her oldest son's bedroom and looked out that window, again it stopped.

She got back to bed and heard it again. Annoyed that it was keeping her up, she pulled on some sweats, went downstairs, determined to find what house had the dog. When she came down the stairs and around the corner to the kitchen, she saw the fire shooting out of the outlet near the stove.

She ran up stairs waking the boys and getting them out of the house as her youngest son called 911. While the firemen worked to save the home, the neighbors gathered to give support. She asked who had the dog; his barking saved their lives and she wanted to thank the owners.

No one in the area owned a dog. She must have imagined she heard barking. One of the neighbors suggested that the crackling of the fire must have sounded like a bark. It was just her imagination they told her.

The house was saved with only minor damage to the kitchen. The fire chief told her the batteries in the smoke detectors were corroded and need to be replaced. He also told her, "You were lucky you saw the fire when you did, if you hadn't, there is no way you would have gotten out in time; the fire would have blocked your escape down the stairs—that is, if the smoke had not gotten to you as you and your sons slept."

There was no going back to sleep after all of the

excitement and she wanted to have an electrician check all of the wiring in the house. They started the clean up that morning and she told her sons about the dog barking. The three of them decided to walk around the neighborhood for a few blocks to see if maybe their mother heard a dog from another street. But in the early spring, only year-round residents and just a few summer owners were there. They did not see any dogs, except Mrs. Myer's Toy Poodle, who would never be out at night.

That night, when she finally went to bed, she could not help wondering where the barking came from. She was sure it was not the cracking of the fire. And as she drifted off, she felt her bed give, as if something had jumped onto it. She then felt something cold and wet hit her feet, she realized it was just Coco saying "I'm still here."

Coco with her family.

Whisky, the Portuguese Water Dog

As you might be able to tell by its name, the Portuguese Water Dog enjoys being by, and in, the water. This is because their jobs once were to drive fish into the fishermens' nets, retreive lost tackle and broken nets, and swim from boat to boat with messages to other sailors. These dogs look a little like the Poodle and have webbed feet for swimming. Their temperments, according to a breeder, comes in two types—mild and wild. They love to perform and show off, especially in the agility ring and in water sports. One of the things I read about the Portuguese Water Dogs is that they loved to be petted. But when a human starts petting one, it can be addicting! Their beautiful soft fur, whether it is wavy or curly, is absolutely wonderful to touch.

Whiskey

After starting his life in Chester County, Pennsylvania, Whiskey, the dog formerly known as Whiskers, moved to his new home in North Andover, Massachusetts. He was a "mild" animal and would be a perfect match for his new owners. To illustrate how "addicting" a Porty can be, my friend said that when she got Whiskey, she would have to be in charge of his care. Her husband told her that he was not a dog person. But within two hours of the dog's arrival, Whiskey and her husband were playing on the living room floor together. Even though Whiskey knew that he was a water dog, swimming in Massachuetts can be a cold hobby. So Whiskey was content to guard the rugs and the sofa.

When the summer came, Whiskey looked forward to visiting his "grandparents," Ron and Marie, in Toms River, New Jersey. He loved to walk the dunes behind their house, smell the salt air, and sniff the sand. When his "grandfather" went off on his metal detecting forays in search of buried treasures, Whiskey would join him on his search. He loved his "grandfather," a straight-talking gregarious man who shared lots of stories with Whiskey. Whiskey enjoyed the stories and would walk quietly by his side, pausing every so often to sniff the air.

Whiskey became ill in the fall. In the spring, his owners assisted him as he crossed over. They honored him with a special ceremony in his favorite park. It was a beautiful and fitting tribute to a dog that loved the outdoors.

That summer, as his family gathered for their annual vacation, they all noted that it just wasn't the same without Whiskey. Later that evening, the grandfather quietly and warily told the story of spotting the silhouette of a dog walking the dunes. Something about the dog was eerily familiar. So after seeing the dog several times, he decided to cautiously approach it. As he did, the dog looked up, wagged his tail, and disappeared. Ron realized then, that it was Whiskey, enjoying the beach one more time.

This past December, Ron died suddenly of a heart attack. His family and friends like to think that he and Whiskey are both on the other side, walking together as they always did.

Poogan's Porch

As I walked about the Westminster Kennel Club Show and talked to numerous breeders, I had one woman tell me about a haunted restaurant that they wanted to eat at in Charleston, South Carolina. Unfortunately, they could not get reservations nor could they remember the name. I gave them my card just in case and sure enough they emailed the Web site to me. I followed up with the owner of the restaurant to be sure that the story was real. It is not only real, but is a big part of the restaurant's history.

Poogan's Porch is a fabulous restaurant located at 72 Queens Street in Charleston, South Carolina. Open 365 days of the year, it is famous for its cuisine as well as its sightings—both celebrity and paranormal. In fact, the Travel Channel voted it the "Third Most Haunted Place in America."

Poogan

One of the ghosts is Poogan, the cherished "down-home Southern Porch dog," for whom the restaurant is named. In the beginning, Poogan was a lovable mixed breed that looked like a scruffy version of the animal actor "Benji." He went from porch to porch begging for food. If the mood struck him, he stayed for a while to lounge about and enjoy the scenery.

In 1976, he accepted the position as the overseer of the renovations of a new restaurant. When the day came for the restaurant to finally open its doors, Poogan claimed the position of host and proudly greeted the customers.

By this time, as you can surmise, the owners of the restaurant adored him. He *was* the restaurant so they decided that the renovated restaurant would be named after him.

Poogan passed away of natural causes in 1979, but his spirit still lingers. Customers have said they can hear the clipping of his toenails as he moves quickly through the building. His presence can especially be felt on the porch and every now and then you can hear him barking. His paranormal activities are at home with the other resident ghost in the building, Zoe, an old woman in a black dress.

(Check out their Web site at www.Poogansporch.com to see a photo of the beloved pooch.)

Belly Rubs from Beyond

Rita Thatcher from New Jersey shared this story with me about her mom from Montross, Pennsylvania. She warned me that her mom was very particular and was very sensitive to the spelling of her name. "Be sure you spell it correctly in your story." she warned, "Or mom will come back to haunt you!"

Del Johnsen was an avid animal lover who had seven dogs and six cats. All of them were of a mixed variety, but each one held a special place in her heart. Everyday, Del made sure that her furry friends received lots of love and plenty of petting. When she passed away, her spirit returned almost on a daily basis.

But it was not to visit with the humans she left behind. It was to return to give her animals the familiar scratches and rubs that they so enjoyed. Numerous witnesses recalled that at any time during the day, Del's animals would stop whatever they were doing and gather into one area in the barnyard. The cats would begin to purr and arch their backs. The dogs would lay on their backs in order to wiggle in pure joy as they enjoyed an old fashion tummy rubbing. After a short time, the animals would sit up, just stare into the air and then continue on their business. Del's family knows that to this day, she still watches over all her animals.

Max, the Lovebird

It is only fitting that I add a story about our feathered friends. This is another tale of an animal expressing love from the beyond. Max, the Lovebird, was the only "child" of Karen and Ron Steinbrecher of Wyndmoor, Pennsylvania. Max began his life as the runt of his clutch. He was born with both of his legs splayed and for the first month of his life, his vet had tied pencils to his legs to act as splints.

He was so well behaved that his owner at the time took him to church. Karen worked for Max's owner and he kept telling her about this little bird. She really wanted him, but Ron had other ideas. Finally Karen just decided to bring him home. So Maxamillian William Filbert McDonough Steinbrecher began his new life, one that would be filled with lots of love and freedom.

Max had very good self esteem and thought quite highly of himself. Karen found this out one day when she and Max had a conversation with an animal communicator. Max shared his home with a cockatiel named Smokey. They co-existed but were not the best of friends. The animal communicator told Karen that Max was a "happy, happy, happy bird and that he believed that Smokey was not as smart as him. In fact Max said, "Smokey was stupid, but he would put up with him."

When Max left this earth at the age of seventeen and four months, his loss was deeply felt in the Steinbrecher home. Karen would always ask for a sign or, as she calls it, "Kisses from Heaven" to make sure that he was in a better place. Sometimes those signs would be clouds in the form of Xs, a beautiful poem about love and loss found unexpectedly, or maybe one of his feathers in an unexpected place.

But my favorite Max story involves the Philadelphia Flyers. In 2008, the Flyers were in the playoffs. That Saturday, Karen was home by herself and was feeling a little blue. As game time approached, she decided that she would go search for a Flyer's tee shirt that she had won at a Christmas party many years ago. She remembered that she had placed it in the bottom of her dresser. The shirt had never been worn, but she had saved it just in case. When she pulled it out, she noticed that Max had left a little "poop" near the Flyer's emblem. As only Karen can, she mused that this was Max sending her a kiss so that she would not be so blue. The Flyers won that night.

Max the Lovebird with
Karen and Ron

Sadie, the Bull Terrier

Sadie, the Bull Terrier from Tampa, Florida, had the opportunity to experience numerous spirits when she attended her first National Bull Terrier Specialty Show in Gettysburg, Pennsylvania. As anyone with an interest in the paranormal knows, Gettysburg, the site of one of the largest and deadliest battles in the Civil War, has numerous paranormal happenings and spirits. Since Sadie had not had a chance to read the brochures on Gettysburg, she had no idea what was in store for her that weekend.

Those adorable Bull Terriers featured in numerous television commercials were originally bred to be the ultimate fighting dog. Today they provide companionship and love to their owners. But that love and companionship did not apply to the spirits at Gettysburg.

Throughout the weekend, as Sadie would walk about, she would suddenly stop. A low growl would develop in her chest and she would start to back up as if ready to fight. She would then commence to barking ferociously.

This was so out of character for young Sadie. She had never exhibited any type of aggression before. Her owner saw nothing that would incite her to have this type of behavior, but she strongly believes that Sadie was protecting her from the spirits that she, as a human, was unable to see. It continued all weekend long in a variety of locations. When the show ended and Sadie left for Florida, her owner was relieved.

To this day, there has never been another occurrence of this behavior. Sadie has refused to make a return trip to Gettysburg.

Champ and Scout

My partner, Andrea Martnishin, and I do extensive research in order to find interesting ghost stories for Ghost Tours of America. In the summer of 2008, we opened Ghost Tours of the Outer Banks. That is where I learned of the story of Champ and Scout, the Yorkshire Terriers of Kitty Hawk, North Carolina.

Yorkshire Terriers, or Yorkies, are big dogs in small packages. Their heritage is that of a terrier. That terrier lineage contributes to the Yorkie's thinking that it can take on the world, or a ninety-pound Doberman, if it had too. They like to bark to alert their owners to strangers. The Yorkshire Terrier weighs no more than seven pounds and is a very popular breed among apartment dwellers. They enjoy playing with other dogs, however, sometimes they do not realize that they can not always keep up with the big dogs.

Champ

Champ was the lone survivor of his litter. But he never lacked for animal companionship. It seems that he had a Cairn Terrier ghost dog that would follow him around. Both Champ and his "friend" would even sleep on his owner's bed with him. How did Champ's owner know he had a little friend? One evening she awoke to the familiar sound of a dog sniffing. She looked over and Champ was sound asleep, but to his right was a translucent terrier, sniffing the bed.

Scout

Scout, another Yorky raised on the Outer Banks, actually fought off a ghost in his mistress's bedroom in Kitty Hawk. Scout loves to sleep on the top of his mom's pillow. But one evening, his owner awoke to find a six-foot-tall, thin figure of a man standing at the foot of her bed. Scout saw it too and went charging to the end of the bed, barking and growling.

"I must be dreaming," Scout's mistress thought, so she blinked her eyes, but the menacing figure was still there.

Scout became more agitated and made several more attempts to drive the ghost away. It finally worked, as the figure just vaporized.

The figure has never returned, but just to be sure, Scout sleeps on that bed every night.

The Spirit of the White Doe

There are numerous Native American stories featuring tales of a white doe. But while you may think that these are legends from a long time ago, I recently heard a story that confirms that the white doe still walk among us.

The Legend

The Lenape Indian tribe believes that the white deer is a holy spirit. It could be the spirit of a departed ancestor or a kind soul that watches over you. Souls are able to move from the real world to the spirit world in the form of the white doe. This is one of the reasons that tribe elders always warned hunters never to interfere with them.

The white doe, maybe because of their eerie beauty, figures prominently in North Carolina folklore. The first English child born in the new world was Virginia Dare. The legend goes the Lost Roanoke colonists ended up living with, or being rescued by, a local Indian tribe.

As the years passed, two men of the tribe fell in love with Virginia. One was a young warrior and the other, an older medicine man. When the medicine man realized that Virginia was more smitten with the younger man and would never love him, he used his magic to turn her into a white doe. This would prevent her from being with his rival.

The remedy to undo the spell would be to wound the white doe with a magic arrow and the white doe would turn back into the young woman. Everything was fine for a while until a young man from neighboring tribe decided to hunt the white doe.

The medicine man realized that he had to use his magic arrow to unlock the spell before the hunter's arrow would kill her. But sadly the magic arrow and that of the young hunter struck the white doe at the same time. It turned the white doe into a girl, but only just in time to die.

Many people think Virginia Dare still wanders the Carolina woods in white doe form. A disconcerting detail is that the white doe can be heard speaking in a woman's voice.

A Modern "Tail"

The modern-day white doe tale took place quite recently. I was talking to some women at a business conference, when one of them shared this story.

Her mother had recently passed away from a long illness. During this time, she had been hospitalized at an assisted living facility on the outskirts of a large metropolitan area. It was a one floor facility with windows that basically faced a parking lot. There was no forest, no trees, or any greenery to be found for several miles.

As the woman said her final goodbyes to her mother, she had a strange feeling. It was almost like someone was watching her. She slowly turned to look out the window and there stood a white doe.

"This is so strange," she thought. "How could a white doe possibly get here?" When she turned back to look at her mother, she had passed. She then turned to look for the white doe. The white doe had also disappeared.

This woman could not shake the feeling and mentioned the white doe to one of the nurses when she was leaving. "Oh, the white doe," she replied. "Whenever we see one, we know that someone has moved on to a better place."

Hatteras Jack, the Sailor's Friend

While the majority of this book is about animal ghosts that are pets, some animal ghosts are so legendary that they warrant a mention. Here is another favorite story from the Ghost Tours of the Outer Banks.

The waters around Hatteras Inlet, a popular vacation spot on the Outer Banks of North Carolina, are treacherous and have claimed the lives of many a sailor and fisherman. In fact, the Bodie Island Lighthouse was once known as the "Body" or "Bodies Island" Lighthouse because of the number of bodies claimed by the sea that have washed ashore in that area.

But before the days of complicated navigational tools or Global Positioning Systems, there were simpler ways to stay safe and navigate these treacherous seas. A sailor would follow the beacon of the lighthouses, rely on the help of the fearless lifesaving crews, or use Hatteras Jack.

Hatteras Jack is an all white dolphin whose job it was to help sailors navigate the inlet. He signaled to the sailors by jumping into the air when it was safe to navigate the tide and sail the channel. Sometimes he even led the way!

Word spread among the sailors about this helpful little fellow. Sometimes the ship captains would even blow their foghorn when they reached the inlet in order to request Jack's help. Jack would suddenly appear and when all was safe, would give the signal to proceed. Once the ship was safely through the inlet, Hatteras Jack would put on a little show for the sailors. He would jump, rollover, and even walk on his tail for his admiring and thankful audience.

As time passed and ship's navigational tools became more sophisticated, the need for Hatteras Jack's help declined and he eventually was no longer seen. There are two theories as to where he has gone. One is that he has moved onto other treacherous seas to assist other sailors. And the other is that Hatteras Jack was actually the spirit of a sailor who was finally able to accept death once his fellow seamen no longer needed him.

Emergency Communication

Did you ever feel that your animals were trying to communicate with you but you just could not understand what they were saying? This was the case for Meredith from Kitty Hawk, North Carolina. The following is a story that she shared with me about her two Australian Cattle Dogs.

Australian Cattle Dogs are the result of numerous cross breedings that began in the 1800s. Breeders wanted a dog brave enough to herd sheep and cattle, but at the same time, desired a sturdy breed to withstand the hardships of the weather. It is believed that the Australian Cattle Dog is an actual descendant from the Dingo.

The Australian Cattle Dog's main job in the 1800s was to keep the cattle in line by nipping at their heals. Because their coat can be either tan or "blue," they acquired the nickname of the Blue Heeler. The average life span of this dog, which is about eighteen inches tall and weighs around forty pounds is twelve years.

Today, the Australian Cattle Dog is still used to herd cattle on occasion, but also is a wonderful companion if it has a job to do. They can be a bit distrustful of other people and animals. That is why this story of animal communication is so unique.

After spending a long day at a horse show in Benson, North Carolina, Meredith and her family began the long return trip home. Their horses were in the trailer that they were pulling along with their camper. Her two dogs were in the back of the bed of the truck where they normally ride.

Once the dogs had been loaded into the truck, Meredith got an extremely funny feeling. "Please," she begged her husband, "Let's put the dogs up front in the truck with us."

"No there is no room," he replied. So everybody stayed the way they were and off the family went. As they continued to drive, Meredith became more and more uneasy. Every time she made eye contact with the dogs, her uneasiness grew tenfold.

They decided to stop and have dinner when they were half way home. Once again, that very uneasy feeling grew over Meredith. Every time she looked at her dogs, she became more and more agitated. "Please," she begged her husband once again, "take them out of the back of the truck. I really believe something is going to happen to them."

"You're being silly," replied her husband, so they loaded up the family and continued their trip to Kitty Hawk. A half hour into the trip, Meredith became hysterical and could not look at her animals without crying. "You have to get them out!" she begged.

Finally, her husband relented and pulled over to the side. Greatly relieved, Meredith loaded her two dogs into the camper. Within fifteen minutes, a tire blew on the trailer. It was extremely loud and caused the trailer to swerve all over the road. Meredith looked back at the trailer. She knew that if the dogs had remained in the back of the truck, they surely would have jumped out because of the noise. They would have been killed.

As she looked in on her dogs, they were wearing a big smile!

Remington

Molly

Whiskey

Patty

Leroy

Rush

Coco

Kelly

Jazz

Ghost

Casey

Roxie

Elmo

Harrison

Angelo

Peaches, the Maine Coon Cat

Peaches was a Maine Coon Cat from Pottstown, Pennsylvania. Now, Maine Coons are one of the biggest domestic cats sometimes reaching almost twenty-five pounds. They also have an interesting past with many legends surrounding their heritage. This breed has their origin in Maine, although some stories say that their distant relatives were descendants of cats owned by Marie Antoinette. She had sent her cats to Maine when she was planning to flee France before the Revolution.

Another tall "tale" is that the cats were actually a cross breeding between a raccoon and a domestic cat. This is a story that Maine residents like to share with unsuspecting tourists.

But the story with the most documentation features a Sea Captain named Captain Coon who smuggled a long-hair cat on his boat to assist in the rat patrol. The cat found a safe haven to have her litter at a farmhouse in Maine and the line of Maine Coon cats was born.

Despite their size, Maine Coons are energetic and active cats. Peaches had white paws and a grey, black, and white nose and very thick fur. In fact, her long dense fur gave her the appearance of a little lion.

According to her owners, Peaches was "a character." She only drank water out of faucet and only ate dog food. That is of course unless tuna fish was available. She used to love to run across the kitchen floor, but she always let her tail drag across it. Her owner thought this was a neat trick—it was like have their own furry feather duster.

When she was fourteen years old, Peaches passed away. One week later, her owner looked down and there she was—scampering across the kitchen floor. "Peachy Girl, where are you going?" her owner asked. But Peaches was on a mission. With just a quick glance back, Peaches, with her tail on the floor as it always was, trotted away and disappeared.

Lovely Lucy, the Abyssinian

The Abyssinian is a very people-oriented breed of cat. They are very playful and energetic with a rich coat and a lean athletic body. Lucy, the Abyssinian, owned by Angela and Ron Megasko of Glenmoore, Pennsylvania, was true to this breed description. When I asked Angela to describe Lucy she said, "She was a little sprite. Her happy feet enabled her to be everywhere all at once. She was this way in her life, and even after she left us."

The Megaskos decided on an Abyssinian after a visit to a local cat show. It was a wonderful breed that they felt would fit into their household. They also thought a more playful cat would be a good companion for their aging cat, Gabby. So they made an appointment and went up to see a breeder in Clarkside, Pennsylvania.

Originally they were interested in purchasing Lucy's brother. But as they watched him racing around the room and running into the walls, they thought, "He might have a bit too much energy for us."

Out of the corner of their eyes, they saw Lucy. She was still playful, but had that air of dignity about her. She looked at the Megaskos as if to say, "My brother is crazy, but I am the girl for you."

After much convincing, the breeder sold Lucy and she began her life in Glenmoore.

Lucy loved to play. She was always busy, batting at a bathrobe tie or a toy. Born in March, Lucy was a true Pisces. She loved the water and enjoyed having a bath, an anomaly for a feline. If someone else decided to take a bath, she was right there to assist them and to test the water coming out of the spigot. In the morning, Lucy was right there to wake everyone up. It was like she had her own kitty "To Do" list. She was ready and willing every morning to take on the world.

I had the pleasure of meeting Lucy many years ago. We had been invited to have dinner at the Megaskos. It was the first time we were ever going to their home. After a wonderful meal, we were sitting in the dining room enjoying some dessert and good conversation. The Megaskos' dining room is separated from their living room by glass doors. As I looked into the living room, I saw a cat, taking my wallet out of my purse, which I had left on the chair. As I watched, the cat had actually opened the wallet and was beginning to take out my credit cards.

"Angela," I said, "what is your cat doing?"

"Oh, that is Lucy," she replied. "I taught her to take only the platinum ones."

When Lucy was thirteen years old, she became extremely ill. The Megaskos worse fears were realized when they learned that Lucy was in renal failure. But as most pet owners know, during this time, you really do not know what to do. How much pain is your pet in? What do they want you to do? You want to do what is best for them, but you love them so much, you just don't want them to go. Did Lucy want to move on to her next assignment? Or should they continue to try to keep her alive by heroic means?

At this point in time, the Megaskos decided that they wanted to speak with an animal communicator to help them help their beloved Lucy. The animal communicator asked several questions to confirm that she was speaking to Lucy. One question was about her housemate and fellow kitty, Robert. When asked to describe him, Lucy said, "He was a big boy, slow and a little dumb. He always was a bother." This actually described Robert perfectly. When the animal communicator asked Lucy what did she see, her reply was, "People rushing, people growing, a very busy household."

Since Angela's company, Market Viewpoint, is one of the top marketing research, training, and mystery shopping companies on the East Coast, there is always something going on related to business in their home. At this point, both the communicator and Angela believed that they were talking to Lucy.

Lucy then told the communicator that she really

loved Angela and Ron and she sensed that they needed to have her in their lives. They needed her positive energy and positive spirit to get them through some difficult times. This really resonated with Angela because, for the past two years, she had been dealing with very difficult family health issues. But, Lucy continued, she now sensed that Ron and Angela were not being honest with themselves. She was going to die, she understood that and said that: "Pain was a part of dying and soon it would be over."

Angela and Ron desperately wanted to help Lucy and asked if there was anything that they could do. She said, "Love me, touch me, sing to me, sing me on my way." This made perfect sense to Angela because Lucy had always been a cat that only liked light touches and soft pets. She did not like to be held or cuddled. While Lucy had requested that she pass from this world naturally and without assistance, it became apparent several days later that she was truly suffering. With their love and compassion to guide her on her way, Lucy was helped to pass to the other side.

For a week or two after Lucy's passing, her residual energy could be experienced throughout the house. Glimpses of her could be seen out of the corner of their eyes. They heard her jump off the counter, where she was not allowed to be in life.

But after a very short time, Angela and Ron felt a little tug on their hearts which meant to them that it was time for Lucy to move on. Their very busy cat had more on her "To Do" list to get to and she needed to move on to give her gifts to someone else. Lucy had so much love to give, it was now going to be someone else's turn to receive her wonderful positive energy.

Lucy getting ready for a day of yardwork.

Cats on Tour- Are They Ghosts or Just Troublemakers?

During the month of October, we are very busy hosting ghost tours in Phoenixville, Pennsylvania. Last year, I was in charge of a 9 pm tour the weekend of Halloween. The weather was chilly as it is in October in Pennsylvania, but a group of twenty people ventured out on Sunday evening to hear about the ghosts that inhabit the downtown area.

As we began the trek up to the Phoenixville Library, the most haunted location in Phoenixville, I always stop the group at a house that has been abandoned for at least two years. I tell the story about the ghosts at the Forge Theatre which used to be a funeral home. Over the years, we have had numerous orbs at the abandoned house site so we invite the group to take photographs of the house. In fact, several weeks before, one of the attendees caught a picture of a face in the window. I also use the time to talk about animal ghosts.

As I was speaking that night, out of no where, ran a black and white cat. Of course it scared the group and we all joked that I had paid the cat for his participation in the tour. The cat decided to stay for the entire presentation and then just as mysteriously, disappeared.

Our group went on to visit the Phoenixville Library.

On the way back, approximately twenty minutes later, we stopped at an old Victorian Home to learn about the Charlestown Cemetery. As I began my talk, I looked at my group and noticed that they are not paying a bit of attention to me. Slightly annoyed, I turned to see what they are looking at, and believe it or not, it was the cat. Now this time, he decided to sit on the porch railing to listen to the story. Later, when I finished the story, he was gone. No one saw him leave and even though numerous pictures of the cat were taken, his image was not recorded.

While this cat story was a bit spooky, it was good for business. The next evening at 9 pm, I had several attendees tell me they had heard about what happened the night before. Not sure what they were talking about, I questioned them. They leaned over and said, "We heard about the cat last night and we are hoping he shows up again."

One of the unusual things tourists can expect when they take the Outer Banks ghost tour, is a visit by several cats, both normal and paranormal. We noticed these felines when we were researching information for our tours and when we did our preliminary walk around. Cats would appear out of no where and then disappear. You would feel the presence of a cat at your feet, but there was none there.

But the biggest feline presence of them all is located at the White Doe Inn. We stop at the White Doe Inn because it has a ghost and we also like to tell the legend of the white doe there. Every time a tour arrives at the inn, a huge marmalade cat named "Peace Train" will put in an appearance. He might follow the group for a while; he may just sit in the road and look at them. But there are many times when people will feel a cat's tail brush against them or they will hear a meow, but there will be no cat there.

The cats of Roanoke Island can also experience ghosts or hoodoos that are located on Mother Vineyard Road. One Saturday evening around 2 am, a group of college students were sitting out on the dock, enjoying the early morning quiet. Suddenly they heard a crashing noise coming down the hill. Knowing the rumors of ghost and hoodoos that inhabit the area, they cautiously went to see what was happening. But while they could hear the noise, there was nothing there.

Then they saw a cat spitting and clawing at the air like it was trying to get at something. Finally when the noise stopped, the cat made one more lunge at its intended victim. Then both the cat and the students decided to call it a night.

Blackie- Cat or Carpenter?

Sometimes we can get a story for a book in some unusual places. While I did most of my research at dog shows, sometimes stories also cropped up in bars. One Sunday afternoon last fall we were in a local pub watching the football games and enjoying some libations. I was explaining to my friends what a difficult time I was having securing stories for this book. Now this particular establishment on the banks of the Perkiomen Creek in Perkiomen Township, Pennsylvania, has what one would describe as a "rough clientele." As I continued to explain my situation, I felt one particular character leaning a little closer to hear what I was saying. Finally, after about ten minutes, the gentleman got off his bar stool and wandered over. "Excuse me," he said, "But do you know something about ghosts?" I explained about our ghost tours and about this book. He then began his story.

It seems my new friend was in the contracting business and specialized on doing repairs for older homes. Many times the owners of these homes would complain that their homes were inhabited by ghosts. When he would begin to do the work, he would find that more often than not, the ghost was a mouse in the attic or faulty wiring. He explained that if you are sitting on the second floor and you hear a mouse in the attic, it will sound almost three to four times louder because of the vibrations through the walls. But his situation was quite different.

He explained that one day, when he was doing work around his house, he noticed a small black kitten. The kitten would wander around his tools and then disappear. He assumed that the kitten just wandered off. But then the kitten began appearing in other locations. He was doing a job five miles away from his home and there he was again. The kitten would walk around his tools and then disappear. At another job, even further away, there he was.

This confused handyman searched everywhere to be sure that the kitten was just not climbing into his truck and following him to different locations.

When the kitten showed up again at his house, he decided that he was going to have to see where the kitten went in order to solve the mystery. He watched the kitten carefully, saw him walk around his tools and then right before his eyes, the cat disappeared into thin air.

Tucker- I'm Back!

Do Cats Have Nine Lives?

Is there some truth to this statement or is it a legend? If the answer to this question is yes, that may explain why cats can experience what can be perceived as a mass trauma and be able to walk away with minor, if any injuries. For example, if a cat falls from a high place, it may survive the fall, while a human may not. One reason that a cat may not abstain injury is that it will fall landing on all four feet, bending their legs when they touch ground. They also have a much better sense of balance and are able to right themselves if they are falling upside down. Being much smaller than humans, they also have a lower body weight.

Another explanation for this "legend" is that it refers to Pasht or Bastet, the cat-headed Goddess of Egypt. She was supposed to have nine lives. This next story is one where you can determine if this kitty decided to come back for another life. His owner sure thinks he did.

Tucker's Grand Plan

While I was interviewing dog owners at the Westminster Kennel Club Dog Show I ran into a woman named Judy Hartley from Marionville, Pennsylvania. She said that she had a story to tell, but that it didn't involve a dog. Since I was interested in all kinds of animal ghost stories I asked her to tell it to me.

Tucker, the cat, was a very spoiled kitty. He had all the food and love that he could possibly want. But every now and then he did enjoy a good break for freedom.

Most pet owners know that those breaks for freedom can come at very inopportune times. A break for freedom happens when a package is delivered and you open that door just a little wide in your excitement. *Whoosh*—there goes your couch potato dog or cat. Or maybe company arrives and you have to say, "Hurry in so the cat doesn't get out—then *whoosh,* off they go."

Tucker, especially when he got older, enjoyed being wrapped in a warm, fleecy blanket and being carried around. So it was a great shock that day he escaped. Unfortunately, it was to be his last great escape. He was tragically killed, when a car backing out of the driveway, ran over him. He was eighteen years old when he passed.

Three and a half years later, it was a beautiful fall day and Judy decided she wanted to go horseback riding. She went to a farm a couple hours away from home where she'd previously ridden. As she was returning from her ride, she saw a group of people surrounding a horse trailer.

"What is going on?" she wondered. As she moved closer and peered under the trailer, to her great surprise she saw a little kitten. He was a carbon copy of Tucker.

Judy had not gotten another kitten after Tucker's tragic death. To her, he was the absolute best cat in the world and there was no replacing him. She felt so strongly that this kitten was Tucker. She knew in her heart that he had returned to her. So she decided that she was going to rescue the kitten.

The kitten had other ideas. It was a feral kitten, one that was born to a wild mother and had not had any human contact. As Judy crawled under the trailer to get the kitten, it backed off and began clawing at her. But Judy was not going to be discouraged. She wanted that kitten—she knew that it was Tucker. The kitten, who had no intentions of getting caught, was able to escape and run away.

Judy left the farm, disappointed and in a strange way excited that Tucker had returned to her. So she called the owners of the farm to ask them to keep a look out for the kitten. She even offered a $50 reward to anyone who could catch him.

A week or two later, she got the call. The kitten had been caught, but he was not happy. Judy rushed to the farm, ecstatic that she would be reunited with her long-lost friend. After a very rough start and many scratches to Judy, she is even surer now that this little kitten, named Bushy, is her longtime friend Tucker.

How can she be so sure that this kitten is Tucker? Besides the physical resemblance, the once wild kitten now loves to sleep on a fleecy blanket and prefers being carried in Judy's arms.

Cassie and Yoda

Since I am allergic to cats, I have to be contented with having numerous "godcats." Two of my favorites were Cassie and Yoda. Owned by a very special person, these cats had rough beginnings, but went on to live wonderful lives. Since I can not tell their stories as well as their owner Kathy Blumenstock can, I asked her to write a bit about them. In her words:

Cassie

Cassie was a pastel calico, born with just one eye. She had been a feral cat in Virginia before being rescued, but she never lost her basic shyness despite becoming an indoor-only cat. Her special skill was predicting the weather, always slinking low to the floor and hiding in her "weather station," a wicker basket turned on its side, whenever she sensed rain coming. She always came out after the storms passed, and she was never wrong.

Her passing the day after Valentine's Day in 2000 left a gap for me and her foster brother, Yoda. I grieved that I would never again see her shadowy form hop up to the bedroom window late at night as she spied on the nighttime critters and noises. I knew that I would miss her leaping onto my bed and curling up into a warm purring circle near my knees.

But a month or so after losing Cassie, when I was suffering from the flu, I woke during the night to see her stretched on the windowsill, peering into the darkness. I drifted to sleep feeling a soft lump of fur next to my legs. My other cats slept in their own beds, and did not like to share with me, so I knew it was Cassie, comforting me when she knew I didn't feel well, and letting me know she would always be at hand.

Yoda

Yoda, a striped tabby boy, was mauled by a pit bull as a kitten and left for dead. He was rescued by a vet's assistant whose spouse worked with me. "You already have one one-eyed cat and this kitten has lost his eye. If we get him a home, the vet will do the work for free, otherwise he'll be put down," Sally told me. Naturally I brought Yoda home, assuming he would bond with Cassie over their myopic common trait.

Despite his youth, Yoda let Cassie know he was the boss—and a tattletale. If Cassie got sick, if the mailman left a package at the door, if a pigeon landed on the deck, Yoda announced it. An expert on spotting bugs, Yoda would alert me if he saw a tiny spider on the ceiling, even if it was 4 am and my home was in darkness. A determined lap cat, Yoda often parked himself on me while I knitted or did needlepoint, both of which he helped with by squashing the yarn or making a pillow out of a skein. Pay attention to ME, he seemed to say, even as he proudly posed next to a needlepoint cat pillow he claimed as his own.

Yoda's passing at age ten in December 2003 was a jolt, as he had weathered many problems. But he could not beat the cancer that suddenly had invaded his mouth. After his death, I often felt his presence settling on my lap as I stitched away. Sometimes I still hear his baby-size meow—always a surprise in such a big striped boy—just before I spot a ladybug or spider lighting on a curtain or lamp, proving that Yoda is still on bug patrol!

Cassie the Weather Cat.

Yoda on bug patrol.

Simba, the Orange Marmalade

Simba was an orange marmalade cat owned by a lovely couple in a city in Northeastern Pennsylvania. One of Simba's favorite activities was to jump from the television stand to the chair—and make a loud thump in the process. Unfortunately Simba, at the very young age of one and a half, became very ill and suddenly passed away.

Several days after Simba's passing, his owners were outside on their patio, relaxing. In fact, his dad was so relaxed, he was beginning to doze in a large chair which was located next to two rocking chairs. All of a sudden, a loud "thump" startled him awake.

There was nothing around, nothing had fallen, but the rocking chair was slowly rocking back and forth.

It seemed Simba had come back again.

The Cat of Cape May

In the beginning as I struggled to secure stories about animal ghosts, my editor, Dinah Roseberry, who is the author of several books on the paranormal including *The Ghosts of Valley Forge and Phoenixville*, said that she had one to share. It seems she and another author and paranormal investigator Laurie Hull from Delaware County Ghosts encountered a ghost cat at Elaine's Haunted Mansion in Cape May, New Jersey. The following is a shortened version of their experiences. For a more detailed version of the story, I would encourage you to read the *Cape May Haunts* by D. P. Roseberry.

Elaine's is a well known landmark in Cape May, famous for its fabulous dinner theater, inn, and restaurant. It also is home to a ghost named Emily, a little girl who passed away in the house at the young age of thirteen. The story goes that Emily had a long illness. Her family vacationed in Cape May, but eventually moved there so the little girl could be near the healthy sea air. Over the years, there have been many accounts of Emily's haunting of the inn. Guests of the inn and local residents have shared numerous stories about Elaine's and the stories are featured on Cape May ghost tours.

One evening, under the supervision of the owner of Elaine's, Ron Long, Laurie and Dinah tried to make contact with Emily. As she her communication process, Laurie had the definite feeling of a presence. Both she and Dinah had the traditional feelings of a heavy presence, a cool breeze blowing through the room, and the hair on the back of their necks beginning to rise.

But Laurie was not only feeling the presence of a human spirit, she kept hearing and seeing a cat as well. According to Laurie, she kept getting the feeling that the cat was very close to someone in the inn. She envisioned the cat sitting close to someone and being someone's dear pet.

Ron informed her that cats had always been attracted to the inn. In fact, there were numerous feral cats that lived in the area. But Laurie said, "No—this was not a feral cat, but definitely someone's pet."

Now Ron had never heard about someone in the inn having a cat, but he did confirm that Emily had loved animals. He also told them that the property was located on land where horse farms used to stand. By reason of deduction, he said that horse barns usually have barn cats to keep away the vermin. So maybe she was experiencing the spirit of a barn cat. Laurie continued to insist that there was definitely the presence of a cat in the inn and that cat was someone's pet.

As time passed, Laurie and Ron continued to talk about the inn and the history of rooms. Suddenly, out of the corner of her eye, Dinah saw her first ghost. It was the cat! It was grey in color, ran low to the ground, and moved quickly through the room and around the door jam. Dinah was thrilled and excitedly proclaimed her sighting to Ron and Laurie. At this point, Laurie had become accustomed to the presence of the cat. Nonchalantly she said, "He's all over the place."

Laurie began another EVP session. (According to the Chester County Paranormal Research Society, "an EVP or Electronic Voice Phenomena is where paranormal voices or sounds can be captured on audio recording equipment." The recording equipment can be as simple as a tape recorder.) Almost as soon as the session began, the cat made another appearance.

First he popped into Dinah's mind. Since you are encouraged to keep your mind open during these sessions in order to receive these "messages," Dinah reported that she had envisioned the cat. Laurie confirmed that she definitely felt the cat's presence. Slyly she meowed, in the same way the cat would, in order to demonstrate how he was trying to communicate with the participants.

As the cat's presence continued to permeate the sessions, Ron felt that he needed to tell Dinah and Laurie the story of Room 6. It seems guests were staying in the room and their two teenage daughters were staying in an adjoining room. When their parents awoke one morning, they found themselves covered with feathers.

They were not feathers as those found in a goose-down pillow. Instead they were long, big, white feathers. For a long time after, housekeeping would come into Room 6 and find piles of feathers. The feathers would not be scattered all over the room, they were be placed in a neat little pile.

Dinah, experienced from having a family cat, asked "Could it be the cat was bringing in bird feathers as gifts?" Most cat owners have had the experience of their cats bringing in little treats from the outside for them. But what can be a treat for a cat, such as a caught mouse or bird, can make the cherished owner uneasy. Since the cat was a reoccurring presence in the house, this could be his way of thanking the presence owners or just keeping them informed that he was around.

As Ron and Dinah continued to discuss the potential meaning of the feathers, Laurie remained eerily quiet. Finally she said, "Do you want to hear something really bizarre? Yesterday, in my house in the living room, I found a pile of purple feathers. It was so strange because I had no idea where they came from. We have a bird, but he's yellow and blue. But these were big purple feathers. We have nothing in our house that has purple feathers. I just thought it was some odd thing; that they just appeared out of no where."

Laurie concluded that she had been given a sign prior to coming that "someone" knew she would be visiting.

Could that someone have been the cat or was it another spirit offering a welcome?

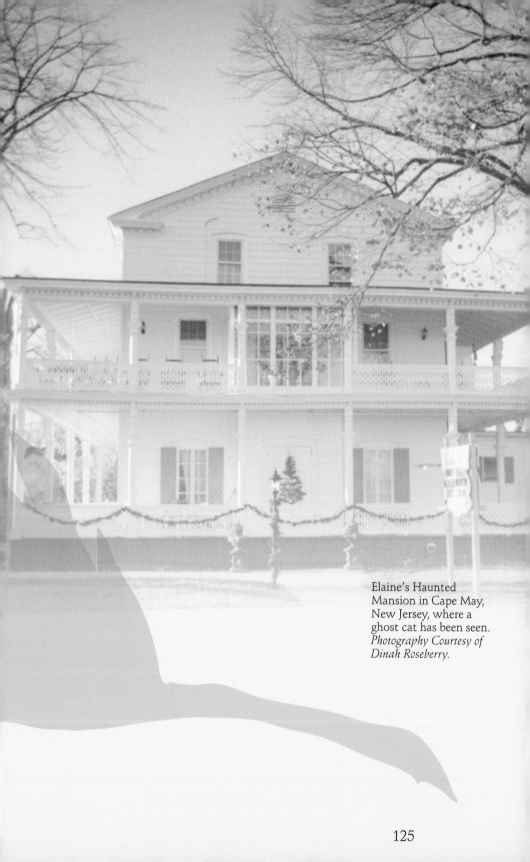

Elaine's Haunted Mansion in Cape May, New Jersey, where a ghost cat has been seen. *Photography Courtesy of Dinah Roseberry.*

Cassie

Lucy

Yoda

Appendix: More to Learn

Doggy 101

Since so many of the dog ghost stories are told by
dog breeders, I felt it was important for the reader to
understand and appreciate some of the inside world
of dog breeding. I have been a dog breeder for over
twelve years. It has brought me much joy and, in the
beginning, great heart break. The breeders in these
stories are not in it for the money. Their love and
dedication to their animals is unsurpassed. These are
not the breeders who you are going to find featured
in an expose on Oprah. The breeders in our animal
ghost stories have their dogs tattooed on their shoul-
ders, have generations of their pets in their homes,
almost always have an animal sleeping in bed with
them, and consider their animals to be their children.
Their puppies are raised in a bedroom or a kitchen
with the owner sleeping on a blow-up mattress on
the floor. I know—been there; done that!

Breeders often will talk about "foundation stock"
or a "foundation bitch". This is the male and female
or just the female that they will use to begin their
kennel. Many times they are not the "perfect" animal,
but with a careful selection of partners, the breeder
will achieve the quality of pet that they desire. For
example, I breed Jack Russell Terriers. When people
think of Jack Russells, they may envision the well
behaved Wishbone or Eddie of *Frasier* fame. But in
reality, Jacks can be aggressive, hyperactive, and
sometimes down right mean. We wanted to breed

a kinder and gentler Jack. Our male, Walker, was adorable and sweet, almost like a stuffed toy. He was the only puppy that survived in his litter. But he had one of the worse coats for a Jack Russell. Jacks' coats come in three varieties—smooth, rough, and broken. Walker's rough coat was soft and fluffy and seemed to grow almost overnight. In order to produce puppies with the proper coat, we bred him with Twinkle, a smooth-coated Jack. She would become a great mother to a line of fabulous Lighthouse Terrier puppies. Twinkle, besides having a great coat, is one of the smartest and sneakiest dogs I know. She always knows when I am carrying a candy bar or bag of pretzels in my purse and she always beats me to them.

Walker is foundation stock for the Lighthouse Terrier kennels.

Good breeders will do extra special things for the mother dog when she is pregnant or in whelp. For example, Twinkle takes extra walks to tone up her muscles and has daily massages to relax her. This also helps with socialization when the puppies are born. By massaging the mother dog, the breeder's scent is assimilated into the mother's coat and will be the first thing that the puppies will smell. Some breeders will prepare special meals for the mother before and after the puppies are born. Cottage cheese, food high in iron, and even premium ice cream will keep the mother happy and producing milk for her puppies.

To be sure their puppies are appropriately socialized, breeders will integrate them into their household. My best friend has a Portuguese Water Dog who began her life in small home in New Jersey. There were eight puppies, plus the parents and older puppies living in her kitchen area. My friend could never understand why Xena was always right there whenever she was at the sink. We finally realized that her breeder always was doing some type of food preparation at her sink. The puppies realized that the sink meant food scraps, so being close to the sink, meant being closer to a quick snack.

Many of the breeders plan to show off their puppies at dog shows. There are several types of dog shows that take place all year long throughout the country. In a confirmation show, qualified judges, usually individuals certified by a national kennel club, judge dogs based on a breed standard. The judge does not compare one dog to the other. The dog is judged solely based on the breed standard. Dogs will compete at these shows to win points. When a dog earns enough points, they earn the title of Champion. Some dog shows are so prestigious that only dogs that have earned the title of Champion are allowed to compete. The biggest show of this type in the United States is the Westminster Kennel Club Dog Show in New York City. Held every February at Madison Square Garden, it is the second largest and longest running sporting event, second only to the Kentucky Derby. Westminster is so popular because it is a two day benched show. A benched show means that the competitors must remain at the show the entire day that they are scheduled to appear. While it is a long day for the dogs and their owners, it gives the public the chance to visit with dog owners to ask questions and see beautiful examples of many different breeds of dogs. It also gives people, like me, a chance to ask "different" types of questions. The majority of the stories that I gathered in this book were secured at Westminster.

There are other types of competitions for dogs and their owners. Several of the dogs mentioned in my stories have won competitively in agility or obedience. In agility, the dog performs over a variety of obstacles when directed by their handler. They are judged on the accuracy of their performance as well as time. Agility is a great workout for both dog and owner, but can also be a great lesson in humility. After practicing for weeks, when you urge your dog to run through the tunnel and he decides to jump over it, it can be a lesson in frustration. There have been many of times on agility courses that my well-practiced Jack Russell has "given me the paw."

In obedience, the dog and handler work as a team to perform certain tasks. Some breeds perform in herding trials, while other dogs will participate in earthdog trials. If interested, a dog owner can find an activity that both they and their dog will enjoy.

A typical agility course.

Doing agility with your dog creates a special bond and enables you to have some great exercise. Exercise is an important part of communication.

Ghost 101

Now for those pet owners who may not understand much about the paranormal or want an easy explanation to what they may have seen, I wanted to include the Ghost 101 information that we use on our tours. When my partner, Andrea Martinshin, and I first began our ghost tour business, we were story tellers. We were quick to tell everyone that we were not paranormal researchers or investigators. I never planned on being the person sitting in a cemetery late at night waiting for something to move. So for our first year, we worked closely with the Chester County Paranormal Research Society and Dinah Roseberry, author of the *Ghosts of Valley Forge and Phoenixville* on the technical aspects of ghost hunting. But as time went on, we developed our own expertise and, of course, had some interesting ghostly experiences.

So let's start with the difference between a ghost, an apparition, and a poltergeist. Human ghosts are the energy or the spirit of an individual who has left this world. This could be because the person has met a violent or tragic death or maybe their spirit is just not ready to leave the present for the afterlife. In some cases, ghosts are protecting or overseeing their property, especially if that property is undergoing some type of renovation. In our research, we often find ghosts going about their normal everyday routine. Some examples include the postman going about his mail route, the librarian still working at the library, the seaman guiding ships to safety and the Revolutionary War soldier guarding his post. Human ghosts will try to make contact with the living in many ways. They may appear at certain times of the day to one or more people, walk across attic floors late in the evening when the house is very quiet, or even touch someone's hair or tattoo.

Just because an individual does not see the ghost, does not mean that they do not exist. People can experience the paranormal in many different ways. Some people may see the shadow out of the corner of their eye. Others may smell the ghost. For example, a colleague of mine took a ghost tour in Gettysburg, Pennsylvania. As he and his wife stopped to listen to their guide, he smelled a very strong tobacco scent. He ignored it for a while and then finally mentioned it to his wife. She smelled nothing. Finally at the end of the tour, the guide spoke about the special tobacco that the soldiers used to smoke. At that point he realized that this was what he had smelled. Some individuals will feel a cool breeze that will raise the hairs on the back of their neck to signify the presence of a paranormal presence. There are others who are so sensitive to paranormal activity that they will become physically ill.

Sometimes an individual will see something but just can not explain what it is. An apparition is the visual appearance of a spirit that does not take shape or try to make contact with people. It is that black shadow that moves quickly across the room or possibly something shaped like Casper. Many pet owners mention that visual shadows of their animals often appear after they pass.

Now, despite what you see in the movies, poltergeists are not always an evil force; they are more mischievous. They can slam doors and windows, throw items around the room, make strange sounds or noises and may even start a fire. Poltergeists usually will focus their attentions on a specific individual or in a specific location. Employees at the Phoenixville Library in Phoenixville, Pennsylvania will talk about the books that they see flying off the shelves or pencils that will move or disappear on their own. Their poltergeist activity has been documented by camera crews from a local television station and by the Chester County Paranormal Research Society. At the Grande Theatre in East Greenville, Pennsylvania, their poltergeist activity stopped when an individual that worked at the concession stand left for another job.

Another indicator of possible paranormal activity is the orb. Legend has it that an orb is a soul that has never learned how to transform itself into a recognizable form. An orb is paranormal energy that can show up as circular balls or streaks of light in a digital photograph. Whenever we host a tour, we highly recommend that people bring their digital cameras to capture any orb activity. Authenticity of an orb picture can be determined once other factors that can effect a digital picture such as the age of your digital camera, water, pixel drop out, and dust have been ruled out. Our investigators like to take several quick pictures from several different angles to see what develops. Numerous times we have not only captured orbs, but faces as well.

Another unusual phenomenon that is featured in one of our cat stories is the Hoodoo. Hoodoos are three feet tall, dark hooded creatures that are believed to live in the woods in Manteo, North Carolina on a road called Mother Vineyard. Stories have them appearing late at night by the docks and even running in people's living rooms and disappearing into the fireplaces. They are scary but harmless.

Orb picture taken on the Ghost Tours of the Outer Banks tour.

Orb picture taken late one evening along Mother Vineyard Road.

Communicating with Ghosts

With the numerous television shows and books written about ghosts, people on our tours often ask how can they communicate with ghosts that might be in their home. So we always go over some easy basic ways to communicate with ghosts. However, if you feel you have a more intense situation at home, please contact the paranormal research society in your area.

When we were young, many of us worked with an Ouija Board to try to talk to the great beyond. But maybe what we really wanted to know is whether or not that boy in our algebra class really liked us. Did you know that working with the Ouija Board may actually be dangerous? Paranormal experts will tell you that the Ouija Board can be a risky way to open up communication with the spirits. This is because the spirits that will respond to Quija Board inquiries can be of suspect character. If you must use the Board, you need to open it with a positive affirmation and be sure to close it when you are done. Never, ever ask the spirit to do something physical to show its presence. For example never say, "If a spirit is present here, show us by moving that chair." This request invites the spirit onto this plane and you may not want that to happen.

Our investigators prefer to use and have used with great success the pendulum method. Now I know I was suspect when I saw one of the paranormal researchers using this method. I thought, "Hmm, I bet that they are moving that pendulum." Well, I quickly changed my mind one evening. We were doing an event entitled "Ghost Hunting at the Grande Theatre."

The Grande is a beautifully renovated theatre set in East Greenville, Pennsylvania. Ed the owner had told us that the theatre was very haunted and had numerous stories and witnesses to back it up. It also has a lovely balcony that overlooks the main floor. Since the balcony was the scene of numerous paranormal activities we decided to try to communicate with the spirits up there. So I took my pendulum and tour group and went up to the balcony. We sat in a circle, I did a positive affirmation and held the pendulum string very securely between my hands. With about ten people anxiously sitting around me, I held it motionless and asked if there was a spirit present. To my shock, someone tugged on the pendulum. I could feel the sweat beginning to flow down my neck. It worsened when the woman sitting across from me, shrieked, "Did you see that! Someone tugged on that pendulum."

We asked numerous yes or no questions that evening and found that the spirit we contacted was the Ed's nephew. He had tragically passed away in a car accident four months after the renovation of the theater was complete. He had been responsible for the majority of the renovations to the theatre and obviously still watches over the theatre today.

Tape recorders can also be a valuable ghost hunting tool. They are able to pick up Electronic Voice Phenomena or EVPs. What you can do is ask a question and then later play your tape back to see if you have captured anything on tape. Oftentimes, a dog will bark or a cat will meow from the otherside—and this is always an exciting treat.

Another time when we were at the Grande Theatre several of the ghost hunters went back behind the stage curtain to explore. This is where the dressing rooms for the theatre had been located. The next day a investigator called us to play back the tape. To our surprise and shock we could here someone saying very clearly "Get Out."

When Is It Time To Let Our Animals Move On?

It was so obvious to me as I was interviewing people that the wounds and heartache left by the passing of their pets were so strong. This was true even after many years had passed. There was nothing that I could do or say to make that pain go away, and oftentimes, I found myself crying right along with them. The question many people asked me was, "When is it time to let your animal go?"

Today, there are animal grief counselors and books on surviving the loss of a pet. The time following the loss of a pet, can be one of the most devastating periods in a person's life. The grief that a person feels over the loss is real, and sometimes even more devastating than the loss of a human.

But that grief can be ridiculed by people who do not understand the connection between the pet and its owner. How many pet owners have met the inconsiderate idiot that says, "Well it was just a pet; you can get another one." My advice to the person who meets someone with those feelings is to just walk away; don't even try to explain to them the feelings that you have. They will never understand how deeply a person can feel about a pet. This is their loss.

There are many feelings that race through a pet owner's mind after losing a pet, just as when a human passes away. If a pet dies unexpectedly, we wonder if we missed some sign that they were ill. We think: "Maybe if I had just walked them more." Or: "What if I had given them different food?" Even when a pet passes from old age, we still wonder if there was anything that we could have done to keep them with us longer.

Many owners will "beat themselves up," blaming themselves for the death of their pet. Oftentimes, the heartache for them is so great that they close their hearts and say, "I will never get another pet again; this is just too painful."

In my personal opinion, closing oneself off from an animal's love is just wrong. Animals teach us so much and give us so much unconditional love. It is important to remember during this grieving process, that the heartache will pass. Wonderful memories will help you through and a new love awaits you.

There are always puppies looking
for love and a good home.

There are simple things that you might do to help get through this period of loss.

A Ceremony

One of my friends prepared a beautiful ceremony when it came time to assist her animal to pass to the other side. She held it in his favorite park and prepared a white candlelit pathway to guide him on his way. She and her husband shared their feelings with him one last time to let him know how much he had meant to their family and how much he had enriched their lives. While this was a terribly sad time, it gave them a sense of peace.

Some of us may not have the time to make preparations for the loss of an animal. Oftentimes, our pets pass suddenly with no warning. What do we do with the feelings that are left? As I mentioned before, many people choose to do a burial service for their pet at a pet cemetery or at home.

A List of Lessons Learned

One of the things I found helpful is to write a letter to the deceased pet. It gives you the opportunity to tell the pet how much he or she meant to you. Another technique that I enjoyed was to think about what the pet taught you. I then made a little list and put it away in an envelope. Every now and then I come across that envelope and open it, read it and smile.

Someone once told me that there are only so many animal souls to go around. They basically recycle themselves based on what lessons that you need to learn.

Look for Signs

The other day I had a conversation with Karen about Max, the Lovebird. As you read, Max had a very special place in her household, and when he passed he left a large void. She spoke with him often and asked for signs that he was still with her. Karen is a jewelry designer and also teaches senior aerobics. One day she was wearing a bracelet that she had created which had a charm on it that was Max's special charm. As she was teaching, the bracelet broke and pieces flew everywhere.

She wondered, "Was this Max's way of saying, it is time for her to move on?"

Meditation

We talked about this and from the experiences I gained from writing this book, we formulated a plan of action. Karen decided that she would put the charm aside and mediate on what Max would want her to do.

What she heard from Max was that he loved her, but he was now doing other things. He was doing great and he was glad that both she and Ron were doing well. But she needed to speak with him only once in a while, because he had to move on.

She realized this was true, but it was going to be a hard habit to break. Last week, she tried and when she didn't hear from him, she realized that he was busy doing other things and assisting other humans.

Is There An Animal Underground Railroad?

My best friend and accomplished quilt artist Diane came up with this idea of an Animal Underground Railroad. It came about one evening when she was explaining to me that when the Underground Railroad existed, quilters used to leave a quilt outdoors with special blocks on it. These blocks would either give directions to a safe location or would identify a safe house. After writing this book and listening to numerous stories, and through my own experiences, I think she is right. How else can you explain how stray animals will find their way to one special house and not the one two doors down? Or if a cat leaves her litter, it is by the home of someone who will nurture those kittens if something happens to her. Or the house where all the rescue animals wind up and then find good homes? If you are that home, maybe somewhere on your door there is a paw print that identifies your home as a safe house.

A Modern-Day St. Francis of Assisi

In the Catholic religion, St. Francis of Assisi is the patron saint of animals and ecology. Many of us are familiar with him because his figure graces numerous statuaries in our garden. But St. Francis may have been a bit ahead of his time. He is a constant reminder to us that the world of God and the world of nature are one and the same. St. Francis lived his life as a very poor man who gave away all of his worldly goods to serve God. His strong beliefs led him to protect nature and include them in his teachings. He believed in the sanctity of life and that creatures were all equal in the eyes of God.

We often hear people proclaiming their love for animals. But few could be considered as caring and understanding as St. Francis of Assisi. However, there are people that exemplify that kindness to animals every day of their life. This story is about one of those people—Helen Blumenstock of Rutherford, New Jersey.

Helen Blumenstock always had a deep love for animals. It was a love and devotion that was passed down from her mother and has now passed on to Helen's three daughters, Kathy, Patty, and Sheila. Kathy has a deep love for horses, even though there is not one in her life right now. She describes how she thinks that love became ingrained in her with this little tale.

Jerry

Everyday when Helen was pregnant with Kathy, she rode the bus to work. At her bus stop, there always man with a horse named Jerry. Even though Helen confided that she was afraid of horses, she stopped every day and fed Jerry. She would scrimp and save, but every day she would make sure there would be a carrot or two for Jerry. Kathy believes that her special connection with horses started all those years ago when she sensed the love her Mom had for this particular horse.

The Blumenstock home was another stop along that "Animal Underground Railroad." We have already discussed that house. It is the one where stray cats and dogs are always brought, where emergency animal care is always given and there always is room for just one more animal.

Baby

In 1987, several children were playing outside the Blumenstock house in New Jersey. Outside, in a window sill, they discovered a three-day-old litter of kittens. There was no mom cat to be found. The young boys guessed she had been killed by a car or had for some reason decided to abandon her litter. They brought one of the kittens, a tiny black and white one, to Helen's kitchen window and asked if she could take care of it.

"Of course!" she immediately said without any hesitation. But just in case, she called Kathy and asked her what she thought she should do. Instantly, Kathy concurred with her decision to foster the kitten.

"Baby" as the little kitten became known, was fed for weeks with oatmeal from an eyedropper. Baby grew up thinking that she was a human. After all, wasn't her mother a human? Baby always knew that Helen was the reason she survived and thought of her as her savior. They were inseparable.

When Helen became terminally ill, Baby never left her side. She would cuddle up close to her, at times making it almost uncomfortable for Helen. When she passed, the family thought that Baby would pass also because the bond between Helen and Baby had been so strong. But Baby had another mission to complete.

She became a great comfort to Helen's husband. Sadly, less than a year later, Helen's husband passed. Baby then took on the new job of comforting Sheila who was living with him. Baby passed in 2007, having lived for twenty years. The girls always fondly remember their parents and Baby is always part of that picture.

Max

Helen too had a wonderful saying to comfort another person who had lost a pet. She too believed that there were only so many animal souls to go around and that individuals should adopt and help the animals that were in the greatest need. "Somebody always knows when there is an opening," she would say.

To confirm this theory, Sheila reminisced about the time her mom's spirit intervened at a pet adoption. One Saturday afternoon, Sheila stopped at a pet shop to look around and just see who was in need of a good home. Her eyes stopped on a beautiful older cat. "He would be perfect for Kathy," she distinctly heard her mother say. Kathy had recently lost one of her beloved cats and true to her mom's word, "There was an opening."

That cat, Max, now lives in luxury with Kathy in her home in Maryland.

Rescue

Continuing on the Blumenstock tradition, both Kathy and Sheila have had their share of adventures when rescuing animals. Some of the stories I will share, others I will not, because I do not want to get them into trouble. Let's just say that if there is an animal in need of help, those two are super heroes that can pluck an animal out of any disastrous situation.

Sheila can win an award for being in the right place at the right time to assist animals in their time of need. One day when Sheila was returning from a brief vacation at the Jersey shore, she stopped at a rest area to throw some trash away. But there was something unusual by the trash can.

So Sheila edged closer and what did she find next to the trash can? Someone had actually thrown a hamster in his cage away! Sheila was appalled, snapped him up, and brought him back to Rutherford. Did he have a good life there! He actually had a hamster car in which he would zip around the living room floor while the cats, many of who were rescued, watched enviously.

Another rescue took place on Super Bowl Sunday.

Sheila, in preparation for the big event, wanted to make a quick trip to the convenience store to pick up a few things before game time. There, under a car, she found a beautiful brown rabbit that someone had thrown away in the snow. He came home to Rutherford as well as a litter of kittens Sheila found in a recycling bin. Do you think that Sheila finds these animals by coincidence? I don't think so!

My last animal story involving this family of modern-day St. Francis of Assisi is one where I played a small part. Sheila rescued from a certain death sentence Chloe, the Guinea Pig. Now Sheila has had some health issues over the past several years, one being a bad back. So the original cage, which was Chloe's home, was not going to be sufficient. In order to clean the cage, Sheila would have to bend down.

So in order to make things easier for Shelia, Kathy and I decided that we would go ahead and purchase Chloe a super deluxe guinea pig cage. Now this cage came with a hefty price tag, but we said to each other, maybe we will get some good karma from it. Sheila and Chloe were delighted.

So Sheila put the cage together and wheeled it out to the sunporch so Chloe could enjoy the sunshine. With no warning the cage collapsed and Chloe escaped!

Luckily, Sheila was able to capture her unharmed and returned her to her original cage. Extremely upset, Sheila called the store where we purchased the deluxe cage. She explained the situation to the shop. The positive end result was the store shipped Chloe a new cage and let Sheila keep the old one. Chloe now has a supersized villa and we were reimbursed all our money. Talk about good karma!

Animal Message Cards

When we host one of our ghost special events such as "Me and My Ghoul," we like to provide a variety of activities to appeal to a broad base of customers. One of the activities that we consistently find to be very popular is Tarot card readings. People are always interested in what the future may hold for them. Or they may have a particular issue that they are facing and need a neutral sounding board that the cards can provide. Readers become more like counselors imparting the knowledge that the cards provide to assist their clientele in making a decision.

However, one of the things that people often do not like about the cards is that they can provide negative images and information. Being an extremely positive person, I feel very uncomfortable giving anyone negative news. Negative news can become a self-fulfilling prophecy or can provide an excuse not to reach to a person's full potential.

So when we decided to provide card readings at the opening of Ghost Tours of the Outer Banks, I searched for cards that fit my philosophy and personality the most. The deck I selected is called Animal Messages© by Susie Green. The deck of fifty two cards features beautiful pictures and messages from animals such as the elephant, bear, humming bird, and dolphin. The cards provide to the reader messages from the animal kingdom. Ms. Green's philosophy is those animals appear in our lives to restore some balance and harmony. This duplicates what we find in nature.

The cards provide an interesting perspective and each individual can take some sage advice away from a reading. It also can answer questions such as, "I have seen a red squirrel three times this week—what does that mean?"

Over the past three months, I have done numerous readings and have been surprised as how accurate the readings are. The cards also have been so well received by people. They love the beautiful pictures and the thought that animals are actually giving them a message. This holds true for both men and women. After reading cards at a recent business conference, I had to smile when, right before we left, one of the men asked me, "What animals did I have again?"

My most interesting reading came, when I was asked to read for a ninety-two-year-old woman. Her granddaughter told me that she loved card readings and had one done many years ago in Savannah. So I was up to the challenge.

For quick readings, I do a traditional past, present, and future spread. While her granddaughter and her husband are sitting right there, the lovely ninety-two year old selected three cards. When we flipped them over, it is the first time ever I have had three birds in a spread. Two of the birds happen to be her absolute favorites. These favorite birds both represented infidelity both in her past and in her future.

"Hmmm," I thought to myself. "What kind of past does this woman have?" "What can I say especially in front of her granddaughter?" When I finished delivering the messages that the animals had provided, a G-rated version, I asked the grandma what she thought. She smiled slyly and told me that she was delighted that her favorite birds have come to deliver her a message.

Animal Reincarnation

There were several places in this book where pet owners strongly believed that their beloved animal had come back to them, but in different form. They are not alone. According to a recent Gallup Poll, 27% of Americans believe in reincarnation.

Basically, reincarnation is the philosophy that a person can return to this world in another body with another personality. That person usually is coming back to earth to work on issues that have not been dealt with or completed in the present life.

Numerous religions have different philosophies on reincarnation and one can spend a significant amount of time researching the topic. But not much has been written about animal reincarnation. The majority of beliefs, however, do make the point that an animal, if it does return to this world, does not return as a human being. Man is the most evolved of the species and therefore can only return as a man or woman. But there is the belief that an animal can return as the same species or evolve into a higher species if they have learned all their previous species' lessons.

Animal communicator Dinah Roseberry says, "I've been personally involved with animals who've chosen to come back to their prior owners out of sheer love. Additionally, they have special reasoning powers on the other side and their desire to come back is often reflected by not only love, but by need. If an owner truly has need for the animal, that is a consideration that the animal will take. But it is not something chosen with any ease.

"Life on the other side is beautiful for animals—especially if the last days or years for the animal on earth were sickly or filled with pain. To choose to come back as a puppy, kitten, or other baby animal is a big decision. With their prior living owners being such a big part of the decision to reincarnate, humans should try not to be selfish. Remember that you are asking for an animal to leave a wonderful place to return to earth where they will experience—even if well loved—sickness, pain, or other trauma as our lives indicate.

"Animal communicators usually find reincarnations to be a fun type of communication as once the decison is made by the animal in question, there is happiness and excitement about the return. I strongly recommend to people that if they would like a deceased animal to reincarnate, to contact a communicator (or learn the skill) to discuss it with the animal. The last time you saw your beloved pet, just might not have to be the last time afterall!"

Animal Walk-Ins

Just like with animal reincarnation, there is not much evidence to prove the existence of animal "walk-ins," but it is interesting to speculate if this phenomena could apply to them.

According to Ruth Montgomery, author of the popular book *Strangers Among Us,* a walk-in occurs when two souls agree to switch places. This often happens when one soul has learned everything possible in this lifetime and wants to move on to its next destination to continue learning. The new soul, which usually will enter an older body, has new knowledge to impart and/or special tasks to complete. The walk-in will have the advantage of the already up-and-running body and mind to immediately begin its work. The disadvantage is the walk-in has taken over another's life and may not remember any of it. This can be especially difficult for the walk-in that might have a spouse and a family.

The walk-in often occurs during times of great stress such as a car accident or some other near death experience, or possibly a severe bout with depression or suicide attempt. It is said that the two souls strike up a deal where the one can leave the dying body for new challenges and the new soul will heal the mind and body so they can begin their new work without starting out as a baby.

Animal communicator Dinah Roseberry says, "Walk-ins in relation to animals often occur when an animal has been through such harsh circumstances (often in abuse cases that have landed an animal in a humane society), that they no longer want to deal with the horrors of a life on earth.

"This then is the perfect time for the animal who wants to come back to an owner to make the deal with the tired animal for a walk-in status. It's an agreement where both sides benefit. Then, synchronicity sets in. The universe manages a plan that puts the prior owner in the right place at the right time to meet the previously forlorn animal and there is immediate love. Once the deal is sealed (in whatever way this needs to happen, whether it be through a humane organization, a person who can no longer keep their pet, a rescue—any number of scenerios), the walk-in takes place. There will be a time of recognition, but soon, the animal slides into the life of the prior animal with just some of the traits of the deceased animal. It is a new life for the walk-in."

Remember the story of Driving Miss Daisy Crazy? His owner firmly believes that "Angelo" was an old soul. He knew everything about showing in the confirmation ring and did not exhibit any of the traditional behaviors credited to a dog show novice or even a puppy. Maybe Angelo wanted that second chance to come back and become a champion or maybe he is just one smart puppy…you decide.

Final Thoughts
What I Have Learned

There is no doubt in my mind that our animals both past and present, try to communicate with us. But we need to be open to receive those signals. We also need not to feel that there is "something wrong with us" if we experience these feelings. Find other individuals that feel the same way and share your feelings with them. Keep a journal of your communications and any of your animal sightings. See if there is a particular time, as many of the individuals in the stories state, when you see them. But most of all, always keep your heart open.

You never know when your next animal friend will be behind that next door.

"Whew—my paws are so tired from typing this book!"

Bibliography

Books

Fogle, Bruce Dr.. *Dogalog*, New York, New York, Penguin Press, 2002

Roseberry, D. P. *Cape May Haunts*, Atglen, PA, Schiffer Publishing, 2007

Internet Resource List

Carol Gurney. http://gurneyinstitue.org

Ghost Stories. http://paranormalstories.blogspot.com

International Association of Pet Cemeteries. http://iaopc. com

Karen Douglass—All Creatures Great and Small, LLC. www. allcreatures.net

Poogans Porch. http://www.poogansporch.com/legends

Reincarnation. http://www.blavatsky.net/topics/reincarnation

St. Anthony Messenger Feature Article. http://www.americancatholic.org

Walk In. http://www.greatdreams.com/walkin

Wikipedia. http://en.wikipedia.org

Photo Credits